D0001542

CHANGE YOUR

HOME

CHANGE YOUR

LIFE™

ANDERSON

table of contents

Introduction 8

What Are You Waiting For? 14

What Does Your Home Say About You? 28

Every Room Can Affect Your Life 36

Finding Your Inspiration 48

Romancing the Home 58

————— MOLL'S FIVE MUST-HAVES —————

Paint Yourself Out of a Corner 70

Light: Dim & Dimmer 108

Music: The Atmosphere Thermostat 122

Flowers: Petal Pushers 132

Fabric: By the Bolt 146

A New Lease on Life 160

Bachelor Pad, Bachelor Dad 170

Life of the Party 194

APPENDIX

Special Touches: Room By Room 212

Clutter Control 215

Home Away From Home 216

Toolbox Basics 220

The Green House Effect 223

Meet Moll Anderson 224

I have so much to be thankful for in my life, and that, of course, starts with the fact that I have been truly blessed with many people who have supported and believed in me for years. First and foremost are my parents: My mother, Ellen, still the ultimate hostess and the finest teacher of no-stress entertaining, and my late father, William Taft Ruffalo, that most dapper gentleman; I miss him more than words can express.

Thanks to my brother, Bill Ruffalo, and my three nieces, Courtney, Tiffany, and little Molly, for loving me and being excited for me. Karen Hall and Nancy Lacy have supported me always, no matter what corners I've painted myself into! Penny and Richie Brand for their friendship and the gift of their precious daughter Lindsey; she was an angel on Earth and now she is an angel in Heaven. Thanks to Sherri Huff and Susie Reid for your love and support. Kitty Moon Emery, the President of my company, believed in me when I was just a woman with an idea, gave me a computer and a desk in her office, and told me I was great when I needed it the most! Jennifer Willey Taser, my Vice President and dear sister, remembers I'm not just the plate. Amanda Norman is too talented beyond her years and more than my assistant—I thank her for her contributions to this book.

Stacie Standifer gave me a shot at my own column in her magazine *Nashville Lifestyles* and made me legit; I thank her and her whole staff, especially Rick Johnson. To the whole Highlander Builders crew for their dedication and quality work. Michael Gomez for his fab photos. Thanks to my agent Susan Haber and Rebel Entertainment for their belief and support. I also thank the gang at Cool Springs press, Cindy Games and Billie Brownell, for believing I could write this book by myself. Thanks to Sheri Ferguson for her beautiful graphic design, to Kathy Wright for her belief in me and for telling Cindy Games about me, to Deb Staver for her amazing artistry that makes walls come to life, and to Bobbie McCloud for being the best design partner and friend in our business for the last five years. I'm so proud to be a part of the Anderson family. Thank you for your love and support. My son, Michael Camello, truly understands the path that brought me to today. I thank him for his belief and support and for loving me unconditionally. Here's to dreaming, son!

And last but certainly not least, I have been blessed by my soul mate, my best friend, my chairman of the board, my husband, Charlie Anderson. Thank you, darling, for the countless nights you heard my heart and listened to my fears and dreams and for believing in me and putting up with my schedule. I love you forever!

A modern FAIRY TALE

Once upon a time, I lived in a very large, very beige house in Scottsdale, Arizona. From the outside looking in, it all seemed so perfect. Yet I was trying to keep myself from completely dying inside. I knew I had to take action! I was stuck at home, so I picked up my paintbrushes and sponges and whatever colors of paint I had under my sink and started to paint. I literally began to try to put some color back into my life.

Somehow, I knew instinctively that painting was my therapy. I set out to paint away the beige, bland life I had found myself in. Every day I would get up and paint; I used acrylics left over from some paintings I had done a few years before. If burnt umber was the only color I had enough of that day, I made it work.

I'd paint until I couldn't lift my arms anymore! I was afraid to stop. I was going at those walls as if I were taking a sledgehammer to this huge thick wall built around my heart. I was determined to change my life. *I just had to*. Weeks later, with just one or two walls left unpainted, I realized it was working! I was beginning to change. But it wasn't the change I'd thought it would be.

A modern FAIRY TALE

There wasn't enough paint in the entire world to make that house a home—or to fix my marriage. I could make the house as beautiful as I could, and I did. The *house* was lovely. The marriage was the problem.

But after all that painting, I had literally painted myself out of the corner I had lived in for almost seven years. I was on my way to *me* again, living in full color! I'm not Superwoman; I had—and have—a long way to go. *But I opened myself to change.* I was changing, and I was going to start taking care of myself again.

I didn't set out to become single; I was trying to save myself and my marriage. But sometimes you need to find out what's really wrong and face it in order to figure out how to fix it! It was scary to start over again...and, yes, I had to get out there and get a life. But, I decided to take control of my life and move forward. I have no regrets. Literally, changing my home changed my life!

CHANGE YOUR HOME, CHANGE YOUR LIFE

So rest assured that if you want to change your home—and change your life in the process—you are absolutely on the right track. Others of you may be content with who you are, but your home just doesn't reflect *you*, as you really feel. All that matters is that you know that you want something to change and that you want to start today!

Whether you're searching for design advice, positive words to encourage you, tips on how to select a color to paint your guest bath, or ideas that help you entertain in your home with no stress, you'll find them in this book. Or maybe you simply want to make a few changes to update your home on a budget—you'll find those ideas here, as well.

And those of you looking for something more passionate, more exciting, perhaps for a shift to occur in your life, you'll find the impetus for that, too, in this book. You might want to know how a particular color can affect you in a romantic or peaceful way or how you can get yourself out of a rut. If that's the case, stop putting your life on hold! I'm here to tell you that you can't afford *not* to read this book.

Do something, anything! Even if reading this book does nothing more than get you up and going, it's a start. By incorporating Moll's Five Must-Haves—paint, light, music, flowers, and fabric—you can make simple, inexpensive changes that will have a dramatic impact on your home—and life. Pick up a paintbrush, move some furniture around, even play your favorite CD! As songwriter Richard Leigh said, "Dance like no one's watching." Start a process that gets you moving toward something better than where you've been. Action stirs up creative, positive energy, so get the blood flowing!

It's never too late to be what you might have been.

—GEORGE ELIOT

LETTING GO OF THE PAST

I don't believe in living in the past and I'm not going to cry over what might have been. I must share with you what helped me, something so simple yet so powerful. I heard an amazing thought quoted on The Oprah Winfrey Show that made such sense to me. I guess Oprah would call it a "light bulb moment!"

Let go of the belief that the past could have been any different.

Wow, isn't that amazing! I went around saying it over and over to myself so that it would sink deep into my psyche. Say it out loud, *"Let go of the belief that the past could have been any different."* I am still amazed at how awesome I feel when I say it!

Understanding the wisdom of that concept started the process of change inside of me and allowed me to open up even more in order to be receptive to my destiny. I finally said, "Enough already!" I made a conscious decision to change my life that very day. I knew that if I did, I would never be the same again—and believe me, that was a good thing.

At the time of my transformation, I really wasn't aware that I was in survival mode. All I knew was that I was a pale comparison of myself. I had faded away into disappointment and fear. I needed to get the energy flowing back into my soul and my heart! I had grown so accustomed to putting on a happy face for so long that I didn't even realize that I wasn't feeling anything at all.

My prayers were answered. I just didn't know it then. I can't explain it. I just knew I had to paint—and paint I did. It was a physical release as well as a creative outlet.

Remember, neither my past nor your past could have possibly been any different. I had to go through every situation and every relationship to get to who I am today. I am so grateful for it all, the good ones and even the painful ones.

WHAT ARE YOU WAITING FOR?

I'm thrilled to be here every single day! When I turned 35, I had just gotten divorced. I thought, "I'm running out of time." A very dear friend of mine, who was 55 years old, said to me, "Do you realize that you have the twenty years ahead of you that I just lived?" She was right! And she was reinventing herself at 55 and looking forward to her next adventure in life. If you knew how much time you actually had on this planet—a week, a month, a year—would you waste one more precious moment?

We can be joyful, fabulous, and sexy at every stage of our lives. But it's no wonder we think growing older is scary and daunting. We see so many women and men buying into that philosophy, becoming and looking old. We live in a country where age is not revered as it is in other places. But as George Eliot said, "It's never too late to be what you might have been."

Today I'm happily married to my incredibly wonderful husband Charlie. We have a true partnership; Charlie is, without a doubt, my soul mate. When we met it was like we had known each other forever. I am grateful for every single day we are together.

Thank God I was able to let go of my old life and allow myself to be open to possibilities! If I hadn't, I might have missed Charlie completely. In some ways, you could say that all it took was a can of paint.

So, what are you waiting for?

I believe with all my heart that if you change your home, you also change your life. Making any change to your home—that first coat of paint, that choice of drapes, that small vase of roses—means you have taken your first step on a new path. Making changes in your home is a conscious decision that stirs positive energy into your soul! You have begun a forward movement that's good for you (and that's good for your family, too)! Your home—the place of your refuge—reflects who you are. Is it where you want to be? If not, what are you waiting for?

WHAT *are you waiting for?*

WHAT *are you waiting for?*

If you change your home today, *you can begin to change your life.* Why? Because it's a conscious decision that stirs energy up and into your soul! The Asian culture lives a lifestyle they've been practicing for thousands of years, the art of living in harmony, which modern terminology calls Feng Shui. Followers of Feng Shui believe that energy flow in the home and workplace is enhanced by manipulating the environment to ensure positive energy flow called "chi." If this energy is blocked, you can literally cause negative reactions in your home and life.

Whether we follow specific rules about Feng Shui arrangement or not, the principles stand: How we design the rooms in our homes affects who we are and how we feel. We create the life that we want to live, wherever we are, no matter what our situation or circumstance. So whether you live in an apartment, condo, house, duplex, or even temporary housing like a military base or a dorm room, it is important to remember that home is truly where the heart is.

One of the greatest blocks to creating a home is the fear of not being perfect. For years, all we have heard from other lifestyle experts is that to have the ultimate home, you must design it flawlessly or to host the perfect party, you must be able to afford the hot "designer look." Perfection is not a way of life, and style is not about perfection—or extravagance—but about creating an environment that allows you to live the life you may have only dreamed. Sometimes the pressure to be perfect becomes so great that we panic and end up doing absolutely nothing! So we wait. We wait until we can afford to do it right; we wait until we move into our so-called dream home; we wait until we meet the girl or guy of our heart's desire, get married, and then own a house; we wait until we don't share an apartment with a roommate or pay rent; and we wait until the kids are grown.

16

Moll Anderson client

WHAT *are you waiting for?*

So often people focus only on what's missing: the boyfriend, the baby, the money, the dream home. All these things are important, but by dwelling on these situations, people put their lives on hold and miss many of the opportunities and blessings that are already here. Our homes show where we are in life and how we feel. It's true! Your home reflects your soul. Look around: what does your house say about you? What are you putting off; what have you put on hold?

Are you too busy to stop and fluff your pillows and straighten your bed? Then they're a mess when you walk in the door that night—and that mess affects you. Are you too distracted or tired to finally go through those stacks of papers and photos that are piled on your dining room table? If so, you'll soon be eating standing up or using the coffee table again. (Does that lend itself to quality time with your family or friends?) Are your pictures not hung because you hope to move in a couple of months, and you think it's pointless to hammer a few holes in the walls? Pay attention to what is happening (or not) in your home; notice how simple things affect your life.

*They always say time changes things,
but you actually have to change them yourself.*

—ANDY WARHOL

I'm not trying to reinvent you or your home here. I *am* trying to motivate you to stop and take a few extra minutes out of your day and see that by setting a couple of rituals for yourself, you can effectively begin to shift things. It might be a quick pass through the house to tidy up on your way out every morning. It might also be establishing the kinds of rituals that you begin to look forward to nightly, like turning on music and lighting a few candles. This book is meant to help you not only find out what you're waiting for, but also change your home by moving beyond any fears. Before you know it, you'll have a new and beautiful *home*—and *life*!

For instance, have you put off doing things around your house, like planting a few flowers or even popping silk flowers into pots to brighten your walkway? Do you want to fix up that extra room upstairs that would make such a fabulous home office or finally start that new business? Have you been thinking about getting out that can of paint and a roller and painting away those cobwebs on the walls (or in your head)? Maybe you're waiting until your kids are grown someday, or, or, or! We make every excuse, don't we—from "I can't afford it" to "I don't have time."

The problem is, it shows. No matter what your life situation is, if you're not anxious to get home and plop on your sofa, relax on your porch, or crawl into your bed, then *maybe* something is going on—but it can be changed!

I know some of you are thinking, "Well, that sounds great, but I rent and I'm not going to fix up anybody else's place. I'll do it someday when I can own a house." The greatest investment you can make in your life is in yourself or your family— *today*! That's what you must remember,

Moll Anderson client

even if you're trying to get out of debt. You need to mentally and physically improve your living space to the best of your abilities, and you can do it with a very limited budget! It will affect you when you wake up and when you go to sleep. This truly is a small investment with a *huge* return in lifestyle. So, yes, I mean all you renters, too! Just because you lease doesn't make it any less of a home.

I'm not saying that painting a room in your house is going to fix any problems you may have right away. I *am* saying that if you make the decision to start doing something—anything, even picking up a paint brush—it will stir up the energy way down deep inside of you. I promise you that a shift *will* occur, though it may mean that you have to face some things you have been putting off, like letting go of things that affect you negatively. It could be a job that's sucking the life from you or a bad relationship that's holding you back. You might feel like you're drowning in debt or simply stuck in bad habits that keep you from moving forward in your life. *Just get rid of all that old stuff you're storing in the attic of your mind!*

Start small. It doesn't have to cost a gazillion dollars. Think paint and lighting. They're affordable but have an expensive-looking result that people will notice. Remember, even the smallest change can make a huge difference in the appearance of your home. After all, appearances do count.

No matter who you are or where you are, you hold the key to an amazing life. You can create the life you want to live, no matter what your circumstances. Just a few small, cost-effective changes in your home can make a huge difference in your life and in your relationships.

WHAT *are you waiting for?*

Moll

My dearest and first best friend and I lost contact for years. It happens to all of us. A few years ago, I heard from my mother that Suzanne was diagnosed with cancer. I immediately called and it was like no time had passed. We weren't mad at each other for not keeping in touch; we were just so happy to reconnect. She called me "Moll" just like when we were in high school. We laughed and talked about all those crazy things we did together, and we made plans to get together. Our first friendships are so powerful; it's the first time we have the free will to choose. It's the purest, most incredible opportunity we have to learn to trust and share everything.

I always thought it was so cool that Suzanne's home was so livable—you know, kid-friendly—and still uniquely stylish. The Miller's home was full of love and laughter, and they made me a part of their family.

We spoke at the end of summer, and this time it was great news! The cancer seemed to be gone and she was feeling great; we had plenty of time to plan something special.

I thank God for every moment I was blessed with Suzanne to our final phone call when we talked about how much we had meant to each other. We thought we had plenty of time.

We never know if today will be our last day or if this will be the last time we see someone we love. What was I waiting for?

LIFE SITUATIONS

Life is constantly changing, and sometimes these changes are enough to paralyze us—but just temporarily! Take a look at these life situations to help define the situation you relate to; maybe you'll even recognize a family member or a close friend who could use some encouragement. I hope you get a sense, perhaps, of what it is that is causing you to put your life and home on hold. What *exactly* are you are waiting for?

YOU'RE SATISFIED WITH YOUR LIFE, JUST NOT YOUR HOME

Life is good—it's great, actually! You're content with things just the way they are, but it would be nice if the walls were a different color and the couch a bit more comfy.

What's stopping you from taking those first steps?

SINGLE AND SEARCHING

You're single and waiting to buy or fix up your home until you find The One. What's the point of having a beautiful home, you say, if there's no one to share it with?

How can you find better balance in your life? After all, you deserve to enjoy yourself now.

SINGLE AND SATISFIED

You have everything you need—except a house that's as pulled together as you are.

What time-efficient and cost-effective changes can you do to make your home even better than it already is?

DIVORCED (OR JUST FEELS LIKE IT)

You've recently (or not so recently) ended a relationship. Whether it was marriage, living together, or a long-term dating scenario, the end of the relationship seems to be the end of your life!

How can you get out of your rut and move past the "you" who only knows yourself as part of a "we"?

NEW PARENTS

The joy of a little one is beyond expression, but so is your exhaustion.

Where are the time, money, and energy to change your home and not lose your relationship while the focus is baby, baby, baby?

PARENTS WITH TEENAGERS

You and your home have survived long enough to get your kids into the teen years! But everything is outdated. They want their own space, and you need to keep them close.

How do you coexist?

SINGLE PARENT

Sometimes being single means double the work.

How can you create a "normal" home environment and still figure out a way to go from kid-friendly to a dating or entertaining at home atmosphere?

EMPTY NESTER

You never thought you'd have your life back, but now, the last child has moved out and you have more of your life back than you know what to do with.

How do you use both your time and space to help redefine the new you and your new relationship with your home?

WIDOWER

You've shared countless hours in this home. Now your spouse is gone, but everything else remains.

How do you move past the memories while staying connected to the person you miss so much, and let go enough to move forward?

IN COLLEGE

You're in college and loving it, but your dorm room or apartment just doesn't quite feel like home. But then again, what part of a 7-by-9 foot cement cell sounds like home in the first place?

How do you overcome lack of space, not to mention your budget—or lack thereof?

What are you waiting for?

Have you been waiting for someone or something to happen before you change your life or your home?
If so, write about who or what it is.

Name the top three things that consume most of your energy. Are they positive or negative influences in your life?

Think about a time in your life when you were the most content. Was it as a child? In college? Right now?
What was it about that time that made you feel like everything was under control?

Imagine yourself in your "perfect world." Describe it: What is the setting—the beach, the mountains, the big city? What are
you doing—laughing with friends, eating dinner with your family, getting some "me time"? Now write about what's keeping
you from living in your perfect world. Your schedule? Your location? Your attitude?

Name at least ten places in your life where you find love, and don't limit yourself to people!

I always explain to my clients and friends that our homes are reflections of who we are—because it's true. We all want to believe that we're not judged by our appearances, or by the appearances of our homes, but who are we kidding? We are! And whether we like it or not, we do make first impressions and they do count! Your home is a reflection of your inner self, and it says so much more about you than you may have thought possible. Have you ever said to yourself, "If these walls could talk"? Well, they do! What does your home say about you?

WHAT *does your home say about you?*

WHAT
does your home say about you?

What would you say if I said to you that *your home reflects your soul?* Think about it. What was the state of your home when you left for work this morning? Did you make your bed when you got up so that your linens look fresh and inviting when it's time to snuggle back into them? Or is your bed in complete shambles from a night of tossing and turning? Did you wash the breakfast dishes so that you won't dread coming home to them tonight, or are they piled up with dried food on them so that it will take twice as long to clean them later?

A good home must be made not bought.

—JOYCE MAYNARD

Just like our home, we reflect what's going on inside of us. Our souls—our gut instincts—can be a barometer for what's going well and for what's not going so well. If our lives are crazy-busy, or if we're stuck some place, we tend to let things go. Or, it can simply be a matter of poor habits. The point is, we often don't take the time to do the little things that make such a difference for ourselves and our families.

I realize that we are all in a hurry and looking for a few extra moments just to breathe, but you'd be amazed how just a few simple little steps in the morning and at night can really make a huge difference in your life.

Think about it. When you get ready to meet someone new, or prepare for that first interview for a new job, look how much energy you put into how you will appear. The first time someone is coming over to visit, or if you are throwing a

get-together, don't you go out of your way to make everything look great? Of course! But after the first impression, what is essential is that you have the joy to back it up! Together through this book, we will get in touch with your joy so that it shines brightly through you and all you do! Then people's only impression of you will be: *Fabulous!*

We are how we live.

Think about it. Our homes reflect everything that's happening and wherever we are in our lives. If we are successful or struggling, sad or happy, warm-hearted or a bit on the formal side, those feelings permeate our space and affect our lives. I'm sure you've heard statements like, "That home has great energy," or "I didn't feel comfortable in their house," or "I always feel happy when I visit," or even "That house is a bit creepy." We get a real feeling for people and where they are in their lives when we literally walk into their lives at home.

This concept isn't about having lots of money to decorate. You can visit any city, and if you go from apartment to apartment, you will always find a mother who, despite her circumstances, keeps a perfect home for her family—clean, warm, and loving. She creates a soft place for her family to come home to. Her home reflects her heart and soul. It's not full of luxurious fabrics or fine art; it doesn't have a penthouse view or the latest in kitchen gadgets but it's nurturing. Her home reflects her spirit.

So just think about it. Your walls do talk. What do they say about you?

Moll

She had beautiful eyes with a soft voice and the most loving spirit. Margarite Keaggy was my grandmother although I actually called her "Mother." My grandparents didn't have a lot of money, but they managed to raise ten children in a small house. Mother kept a warm and inviting home that always smelled of coffee and cinnamon rolls when I visited. This most loving, giving, and amazing human being had a huge effect on my life (and unfortunately, contributed to my weakness for cinnamon rolls!). Despite my tough, tobacco-chewing grandfather, whom we called "Paka," it was Mother who made that old house in Ohio a home. Left to Paka, they would have had a motorcycle in the living room and old spit tobacco in coffee mugs on tables and counters. What an impression that would have left! Of course, that old house would still have been special because Mother and Paka were there, but my experience of the incredible atmosphere Mother created there is what shaped my memories. It is the atmosphere that has stayed with me and still today says such wonderful things about my grandparents.

I was only seven when our family lost Mother in a tragic car accident. It was my first experience losing someone so incredibly special. My life was never the same without her. Home was definitely where Mother was. But as I look back, I realize that I took Mother with me—in the cinnamon rolls and the warm coffee-scented air. She taught me the importance of creating a warm and inviting environment, and how to have a home that truly reflects one's soul.

Homecoming

What is the first impression your home gives the world? Don't think about it too much! Just jot down the first thoughts that come to your mind. Words, phrases, colors, sounds, aromas—everything!

Have a conversation with your home (literally). If your walls could talk, what would they say about you? Write it down.

Now, what would you like your home to say about you? (Don't think about this one too hard either.) What image do you want to give off? Sophisticated and sleek? Comfortable and laid back? A combination of different images and feelings?

_____

_____

_____

_____

_____

_____

_____

_____

_____

Name three places that you'd like to live besides your home. You might choose anything—a friend's house, a cool apartment on TV, a mansion from a travel magazine, a thatched-roof hut on the beach. What is it about those places that you like so much? Pick an adjective to describe each of your three places. Are these qualities you see in your home?

_____

_____

_____

_____

_____

_____

From the outside looking in

When you go home tonight, walk up to your front door as if you were a complete stranger. Ask yourself some questions about what you see. Observe who you look like to the rest of the world.

every room

Have you ever really thought about how all the rooms in your home are different? Some are for sleeping, another for preparing meals; others are for eating, kicking back, working, or cleaning. Some just welcome you in the door! How do each of these rooms affect you and your family? Our rooms affect our lives—and our lives affect how we live in our rooms!

can affect your LIFE

t's not just about making the rooms of our home *look* fabulous; it's about making each room *feel* fabulous, as well! There is a "purpose" for every room in your home—and that dictates quite a bit how you fill those rooms as far as furniture and vibe—but every one of us has different ideas about what we actually need in each of those rooms.

Just because a room is *supposed* to be a dining room doesn't mean that it *must* be. If a formal dining room doesn't fit your lifestyle, then make it some other kind of room that will work for you. Maybe your lifestyle is much more casual—perhaps you prefer the Tuscan approach—so a big country table in your kitchen is really more practical for your family than a formal dining area. When I entertain, everybody always ends up in our kitchen anyway, no matter what I do!

Remember those great old scary movies? There seemed always to be a room with a door, usually at the top of the stairs or leading down to the basement. In any thriller, the suspense about opening that door and going into that room or basement builds and dominates the screen. Unfortunately, it's not that much fun when the same thing happens in your home! I have friends who say, "Don't open that" or "you can't go in there." It's time to take that room that no one is allowed to see and turn it into a useful productive space!

Start by taking stock of the space you have and what you use it for. Does your home reflect your priorities? If you don't use that formal dining room, why not create a place for you and your family to hang out, maybe even a media space, or a home office—make it work for you. Perhaps you have a "coat closet" that's never used because you live in a warm weather climate; consider turning it into a wrapping station or even a display alcove by removing the door, painting the inside, and adding glass shelving. A closet also makes a great place to hide media equipment.

Or maybe your master suite is anything but masterful—what can you do to bring bliss and some *wow* into your bedroom? Look at your home and decide what you can change simply and cost effectively. You'll be amazed at how just starting to remove the clutter and adding a coat of paint can inspire a domino effect to exciting changes.

Embrace your space. Work with the space you have to create a home that works for you. I'll share some room-by-room philosophies to help you start living in every room of your home. Remember: *You* are the most important person to ever step foot in your home. Make it the space you want it to be, whether that's a sanctuary to ease the craziness of your day or a fun-filled gathering spot for all your friends.

So change your home and maybe even how you live in it—room by room!

Maybe the most any of us can expect of ourselves isn't perfection but progress.

—MICHELLE BURFORD

ROOM BY ROOM

LIVING ROOM

For as long as I can remember, the living room has been the statement room of homes. For decades, it's been the one room where people seem to put the most thought and spend their money as though the rest of the house just doesn't matter. We think that nobody else is going to see the rest of the house, anyway, right?

Wrong! You and your family are truly the most important people who ever cross over the threshold; make your room work for you!

People do crazy things and have so many rules when it comes to the living room. They put plastic covers on the furniture and don't ever let the kids sit on the couch. But there's a reason it's called a *living* room—we're supposed to live in it and on it. Especially if it's also the Family Room or the Great Room. How *great* is it if you don't live in it? It's wasted space! I don't remember being told not to get on any piece of furniture in our living room when I was growing up. My mom, Ellen, was pretty cool about how we lived. Our home was beautiful, but we definitely lived in our living room.

So if you've been keeping your living room static and pristine, it's time to *lighten up!* Ask yourself: Why is it so important to impress everyone else? If you have children, think about the example you may be setting about home and lifestyle. It may be time to kick back and kick up your feet. Take that room by storm!

KITCHEN

The kitchen should be just as fabulous as the rest of your house. Think how much time you spend in that particular room! Our lives rotate around the kitchen; it's the center of the home. Notice how the aromas and warmth of food cooking in the kitchen gather everyone to that warm heart. We all have some childhood memory of wonderful scents drawing us to the kitchen. I learned to cook there, but I also always did my homework at the kitchen table. When I got into trouble, it was in the kitchen where punishment was discussed. I dined with my family there, and today the kitchen is still the center of my home. My husband Charlie and I love hanging out in the kitchen the most; he sits at the counter, and we talk while I whip up dinner.

Whatever size your kitchen, make it a warm and wonderful place filled with more than equipment and furniture. Fill it with love, warmth, and atmosphere.

BEDROOM

We spend one-third of our lives in bed, and yet many of us put little thought into the importance of comfort and sanctuary there. We need to love this room. Of course, the centerpiece of the bedroom is the bed; it's by far the most important element. A beautiful bed can affect you when you lie down at night and when you wake up every single morning. (And a really good mattress is essential!)

Make your bedroom the room you love the most. Think about what happens when you walk inside. Do you want romance in your life? Well, it all starts in your head. (And the head of your partner!) Ladies, don't make your room so frilly that your lover wants to run. I once walked into a bedroom that had lilac floral wallpaper, lilac floral bedding, and a canopy bed with lilac silk flowers wrapped around the bedposts and hanging *into* the bed. It was terrific—for a twelve-year-old girl! But this was the master bedroom of a thirty-six-year-old couple. He had nightmares about the lilacs coming to life and strangling him! So yes, make it the room you love, but the room your significant other will love just as much. Make it relaxing and romantic.

KID'S ROOM

For some reason, many parents put way too much emphasis on controlling the look of their children's rooms. I'm not talking toddlers here. When your children become old enough to express an opinion about their individuality and begin to have their own sense of style (whether you agree with it or not), celebrate this! They are beginning to become independent in a positive way. After all, they need to love the room they sleep in, as well.

I spoke with a mom recently who was trying to, as she put it, "steer" her daughter in "another direction." Basically, the mom didn't like the paint color her daughter had picked. But it's *just paint!* Not a tattoo! When it comes to your children, you need to pick your battles! (Trust me, I know.) Life is too short, and raising a teenager will bring many other battles to deal with, so breeze through the ones that aren't really such a big deal.

Let your children have a part in choosing the design for the space they live in. Helping to make those choices will affect them in a very positive way, and make them feel as though their room truly is their space.

BATHROOM

Cleopatra set an amazing example for women. She had an army of men at her command lace the Nile River with rose petals strewn before her barge. The kingdom always knew Cleopatra was

arriving by the beautiful aroma. She knew how to make an entrance, but most important, she knew how to take care of herself! You may not have a kingdom of a bathroom, but you can certainly take care of yourself as though you do. Make your bathroom your escape and your sanctuary!

Create the ultimate escape. With just a few quick adjustments, you can let the atmosphere of your bathroom take you away from everything. Consider the basic necessities, and then find luxurious alternatives that make them *necessary luxuries.* Spas can be a great inspiration for your bathrooms because they really cater to peaceful relaxation. Rolled towels, lots of candles, maybe even a few rose petals in your bath—pick whatever stirs your senses and soothes your soul.

Start with that counter of clutter! The chaos of toothpaste tubes and brushes, blow dryers, rollers, hairspray, vitamins, razors, and everything else definitely won't contribute to your need for a soothing escape. I've resolved my counter chaos by buying beautiful containers with lids. You'll find neat, stackable containers in all sorts of materials—from sea grass, leather, and acrylic to cool vinyl, wood, and metal. Find that perfect box for certain items, and simply train yourself to toss everything in there before you leave the room. A clean, uncluttered counter at the end of the day makes taking a candlelit bath much more appealing. (Start the kids young by teaching them to put items in the right place!)

NURSERY

When it comes to your home and your baby, there are no rules—go as crazy as you want or be as practical as you need to be. It doesn't take a lot of money to repaint hand-me-down cribs and changing tables. With just a little elbow grease and some imagination, they'll only look expensive. Let's face it: Who is this nursery really for, anyway? That's right! It's for the parents and the grandparents. I've watched countless parents racing to get the nursery done before the baby comes. Don't panic! You have plenty of time. The baby actually doesn't even really make it to the nursery for

months. Most parents I know have that bassinet beside their bed for quite a while.

So go nuts with color or your favorite fairy-tale motif. Make it fun and whimsical! Or go modern black and white—do what you have dreamed of or desire. This is one of the most important and exciting times you'll ever experience, so enjoy every single moment. Before you know it, they'll be growing up and wanting that big boy or big girl bed. Then *they* will tell *you* what they want their room to look like.

Moll Anderson client

44

DINING ROOM

I always knew something big was happening or someone really special was coming to dinner when I saw Mom setting the dining room table. It was the place where the guests or those holiday happenings would converge. Remember this: If you're going to have a dining room, use it! (If you're not going to have a dining room, use that space for something else—but still use it.)

Keep your formal dining room dressed. If your table isn't as beautiful as you would like, then cover it with something beautiful, maybe a tablecloth made of gorgeous fabric. Use more than one tablecloth at a time and combine different lengths for a luscious, layered look. Make sure you have either an interesting architectural piece sitting atop your table or an arrangement made of fresh (or realistic) flowers. Add in earth elements like curly willow. Think *wow!*

When you're entertaining, whether serving pizza or filet, blow it out and use that china and crystal. Light some candles, sit around your table, and enjoy that space with your family and friends.

GARAGE

Sure, this is a room outside your home, but it is an *extension* of your home. A garage is a place where people feel free to pile the clutter of the past and shut the door (although some of us actually put our cars in there!). The holiday stuff, the boxes of memories, mechanical parts, sporting equipment, tools, and everything else that doesn't seem to belong inside ends up in the garage.

But start thinking of your garage as another room in your home. After all, if you caught a stranger walking through it, wouldn't you feel as though they were violating your space? Your garage affects you more than you know. Keep it organized and neat; you can still let it house whatever you want it to. But consider how that space is taken care of. You'll be shocked at how you've been ignoring that particular "room."

Can we talk?

Do you have a room in your house that is your own personal scary movie? What is it about that room that makes you scream to people, "Don't go in there!"? Is it because it's messy, unfinished, a color that you don't like? What is your reason for keeping the door shut, and what does that say about you?

What room in your home is used the most? Is it functioning well for you? What could you do to get better organized in that room or give it more atmosphere? Make a list of the ways that you could improve your life in the busiest space in the house.

Which room in your home is used the least? Is it really necessary to have a room designated for that particular use, or is it just wasted space? What would be another use for that room? If it has a lot of sunlight, maybe it would make a great sitting or reading room. If it has low ceilings, maybe it should be a playroom for the kids or an office (you're usually sitting anyway). Think of other ways that the room could be used.

Pretend that you are designing your dream house from scratch. Create a list of "dream rooms." A spa? A sushi bar? A meditation room? Is there a space in your home that isn't really being used? Turn it into this dream room—even if just on paper.

finding your INS

Whenever I enter an amazing home or room, it inspires me. I immediately go home and want to clean and move something. It can be as simple as rearranging the furniture or changing the lamps from one room to another, moving art around, or maybe just picking up flowers on the way home for a splash of exotic color. What is it that inspires you to make a change? Is it the glamorous cherry-red lipstick of a 1940s movie star? Perhaps it's the serenity of a beautiful sunrise? Or does an incredible piece of art move you? Whatever it is, find your inspiration and act upon it!

PIRATION

W hen was the last time you walked into a home and said *Wow!* More important, when was the last time you walked into your home and at least thought *Wow?*

Inspiration is amazing! It wells up inside and makes you want to dance, sing, paint, do *something* to change your life. You may not know what that something is right this very second, but I promise that by the time you finish this book, *you will know exactly what you want to do!* Open your heart and soul, your mind and spirit, and be ready to find whatever it is that will inspire you. It could be something as simple as a Sante Fe sunset that fills you with awe, a gorgeous pair of red shoes in a store window, or maybe a fabulous penthouse in a movie you've seen that you can't get out of your mind. Whatever it is, figure it out. But make sure that when you do, you say out loud, *Wow!*

The *Wow!* factor is different for everybody. We all have our own interpretation of it—no matter where we live, how small our space is, or how much money we make! You could live in a studio apartment and have more *wow* than someone living in a 6,000-square-foot house. You can live in a trailer and make it fabulous for you and your family!

For most of us, home is our destination at the end of the day. If you don't feel like it's your getaway from the world—if you'd rather be somewhere else—then you need to do something about it today. So how do you make your home a destination that you desire? First, define what inspires you. No matter what it is— the texture of a sweater that you're mad about, or simply the color of hot fudge

Imagination is more important than knowledge.

—ALBERT EINSTEIN

melting over rich vanilla ice cream—inspiration can come from just about anywhere!

Use whatever reminds you of a special place, whether an island resort or a mountain cabin you visited as a child. It might even be that gorgeous home you saw in a magazine. If it knocked you out or evoked some feeling deep inside you, then you're off to a good start.

I'm not talking about spending a lot of money here. I *am* talking about a mindset and attitude change. And it can begin

with something as simple as paint! It's the least expensive decorating investment with the biggest return in lifestyle. Start by choosing one room. Then figure out what you can do to create an atmosphere to help you feel like you are at your favorite destination resort—or anywhere that inspires you.

As you read through this book, take a minute to answer the questions from the inspiration journal in each chapter. Don't stress-out about this. Have fun; there are no right or wrong answers. These questions are meant just to get you thinking about—and craving—some of the things you didn't even know were missing in your lifestyle.

finding your INSPIRATION

The goal is to help you realize that *home* can be the destination you race to. In order to create that destination, you must set up your space so that you can live your life in an atmosphere that has the essence of a vacation. How? It's really so easy. It's about taking ideas from things you love and places you visit, from moments and experiences that have affected you and your loved ones in a very special way. Then literally transform your space to help you create a lifestyle that you have only dreamed of. Your dream needn't start with the whole house. Begin with a room—or a corner of a room. It's up to you. The idea is to start, to make the first changes that will affect your life. I promise you this: If you begin to change your home, you'll be off to a running start to change your life!

Consider this book your own personal workbook. It's your passport to travel through your subconscious. It just might inspire you to make quick and easy decisions to help you create your own destination home.

Wow!

For me, inspiration was easy. I wanted to turn my living room into a charming, cozy space that reminded me of one of my favorite resorts in Scottsdale, Arizona...The Royal Palms Inn. I'm from Scottsdale, so this is a place I frequented. I always felt as though I was on a retreat whenever I went there to meet my friends for drinks or lunch. The resort had fabulous old world charm and incredible fireplaces that were always roaring as soon as it was brisk weather outside. So the change for my home was simple. I aged the walls and antiqued the mantle, and displayed lots of candlesticks I had collected over the years; I mixed pieces full of texture and deep, rich colors. I created my own little special resort that I could visit anytime I wanted, and it was so simple. All it took was an inspired moment from a place that I loved and the realization that I needed to create a place in my home that could feel like the Royal Palms Inn every single morning or night if that's what I needed.

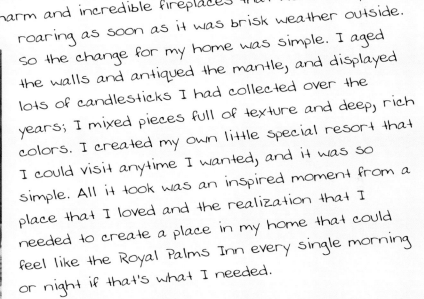

Every morning now when we are at home, my husband Charlie and I have coffee in front of the fireplace, or end the day talking with friends or having a glass of wine in the same spot. It is my way of unwinding and staying connected to my husband, my loved ones, and the things that inspire me. I guess you could call it my own Inspiration Destination.

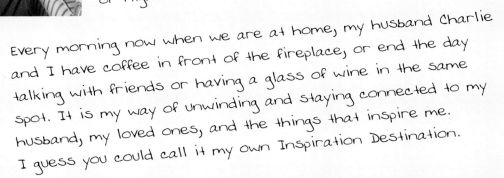

SCAVENGER HUNT

There's a reason why inspiration starts with "I."
It's personal and *individual*.

A color or image that inspires your best-friend or next-door neighbor won't necessarily make your heart race too. That's why I can't tell you *what* will inspire you; I can only direct you *where* to look for it—everywhere!

Go on a scavenger hunt *to find your inspiration*. Think beyond the usual sources; a design magazine isn't the only place to find inspiration (although it is a great resource). In this scavenger

hunt, find at least one piece of inspiration from each of the places below. Gather objects, take pictures, sketch, write in your journal—do whatever it takes to find your inspiration!

Nature

Take a "nature walk." It can be in a park, on the beach, in your front yard, or even down your city sidewalk. What colors and textures are you drawn to? The deep oranges and reds of fall foliage? The muted grays of an overcast sky? Smooth river rocks? Pitted concrete?

Your Closet

Colors, textures, patterns! Your closet is a great way to find what you're naturally drawn to! There you can see the colors and tones you gravitate towards when making wardrobe choices.

A Movie or TV Show

Find a scene where you love the vibe. What is the setting? What are the characters wearing? The year, the time of day, the country? (Tip: Get a big box of crayons. Match the colors to the images onscreen and create a color palette of the scene.)

The Grocery Store

Take a walk around the store. What catches your eye? The bright, crisp colors of the produce section? The cool whites of the dairy aisle? The earthy textures and tones of fresh bread? Maybe it's even the packaging of the cleaning supplies? What inspires you?

An Art Museum

If you don't have access to a local art museum, look in art books or online. Take a photograph, sketch, make a color copy, or tear out a page! What do you find so compelling about the images?

A Song

Listen to a song that affects you. Do an interpretive drawing or painting while listening to the music (think kindergarten!). Feel the rhythm, the melody, the lyrics—what is it about this song that moves you?

A Photo Album

What memories, moments, and times in your life (or someone else's life) inspire you?

The Written Word

It might be a great quote, a love letter, or the alphabet of another language. Photocopy it, cut it out, or write something yourself. Why do you like the words?

The Trash

Off the street or out of the wastebasket, what treasures do you find? After all, "one man's trash…"

Advertising

Advertising is designed to move you! Take pictures of billboards, tear out ads in magazines—what attracts you?

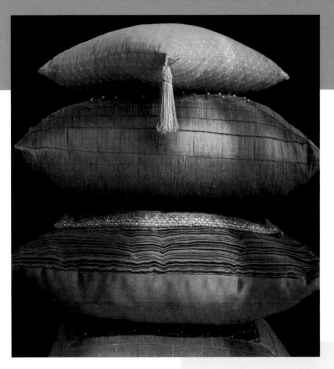

A Fabric Store

Look at all those amazing yards of lush material! Such color and variety. Most fabric stores will cut small samples for you to take home, so pick a few of your favorites to experiment with.

PICK YOUR OWN INSPIRATION

Challenge yourself to find inspiration in a place of your choice. The more "out there," the better!

Collect these items from your scavenger hunt—photographs, drawings, sketches, notes, rocks, old sweaters, discarded treasures, poems, torn-out pages—to create a collage or inspiration box. Take a look at the items as a whole. Do you see a bit of yourself in the items? Are you inspired to make a change?

Add to your collage or box over time. As much as inspiration is individual, it is also constantly changing. Just think about how different your objects might have been ten years ago!

Inspiration destination

Which is your favorite room in your home? What is it that you like about it? The color on the walls? The comfort of the sofa? A particular memory of an event that occurred in the space? What makes you love to live in that space?

Name a favorite memory (or a few—you can never have too many good memories). What colors do you remember? Textures, scents, sounds?

Describe your dream vacation. Why is it your ideal location?

_____

_____

_____

_____

_____

_____

_____

_____

_____

_____

What is your favorite television show or movie set? (Maybe it was a bedroom in a James Bond movie or
the New York loft on the _Friends_ set?)

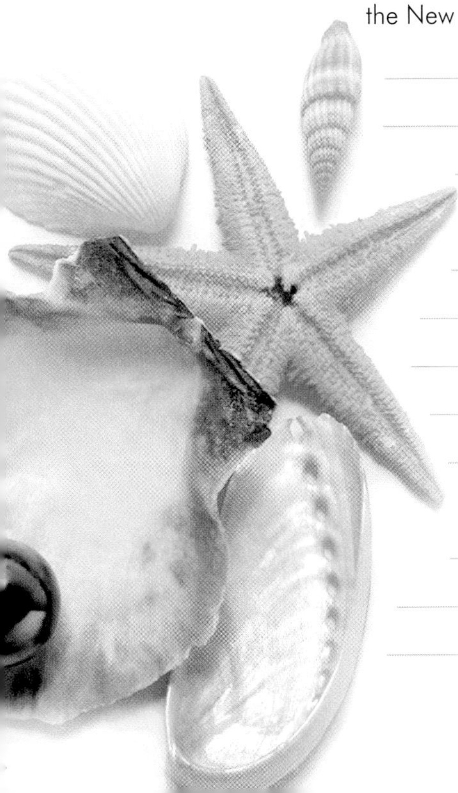

_____

_____

_____

_____

_____

_____

_____

_____

_____

_____

Romance is for anyone who wants to experience all of his or her senses—touch, taste, smell, sight, and hearing—by creating an environment that affects them. It's important to romance your home (and yourself) by creating an emotional attraction—one of the definitions of romance. The more in touch you become with your senses, the more you realize how vital it is to awaken your spirit and live every day in an atmosphere that feeds your passions.

Romancing the HOME

romancing the HOME

Have you ever met someone and thought, "How attractive!" It may have been their clothes or the person's carriage, but something drew you. When I walk into a home and it's warm and inviting and comfortable enough to curl up on the sofa with a fur throw, I think to myself, "This is wonderful and sensual!" I'm not talking about a narrow definition of romantic love or something sexual. I mean the way our senses respond to our environment. A sensual home makes you feel *special*. It's filled with things that appeal to all your senses—you see, feel, hear, touch, and even taste.

By improving the way your home appeals to the senses, you reap the benefits. For years, I held the media responsible for our lack of glamour and sensuality; I felt nothing but disappointment when I opened a major fashion magazine. The fashion models were emaciated and the clothes were so unflattering. And in the home design magazines, every surface seemed cold and hard. Concrete homes with hard beds, no softness or accessories whatsoever, no flowers or plant life of any kind. Homes were unlivable! Sure, they were amazing to look at, but you couldn't relax in them—they were not friendly towards real people, children, or pets. Have you ever tried to recline on a cement sofa without even a pillow?

It was as if the designers didn't or couldn't come up with anything new, so they had to do something drastic and became anti-soft, anti-warm, anti-pretty, and anti-home. At that time, it was very hip to be anti-everything.

But now designers the world over have regained their sanity. Glamour and sensuality are back and bigger and better than ever—both wardrobes and homes! Now women of all ages and sizes represent designers and look drop-dead gorgeous. Home magazines focus on creating a haven that's warm and inviting, relaxing and safe, with exquisite rooms. The fashion designers have jumped on the bandwagon and are creating lines for the home.

Moll Anderson client

So how do you *romance* your house? Start with something simple—just one or two simple things can make *all* the difference. All of us can light a couple of candles, have fresh flowers whenever possible, or *use* the crystal instead of staring at it in the cabinet. It starts with treating yourself well. Which fabrics feel luxurious to you? Make the sheets on your bed as special as possible. (Think about how much time you actually spend in your bed!) Go with thread count that's at least 400 (I prefer 600 thread count). Think you can't afford it? You can't afford not to! I call it cost per living—CPL. Divide the cost of beautiful bedding over those nights that you crawl into bed and you'll find it's a worthy investment with a gigantic return of a good night's sleep, not to mention soothing to your senses.

Only passions, great passions, can elevate the soul to great things. —DENIS DIDEROT

Be able to dim the lighting, and make sure you can hear music throughout your home. You don't have to invest in a great stereo; carry a portable player from room to room, including your bathroom. (Trust me, it works, I did it for years!) Use that good china more this year; stop saving all the good stuff for company. You are the *most important* guest who will ever be in your home!

Remember that your home—and your appearance—reflects your soul. I know if you're a new mom, you're exhausted and you can't find anything to wear that isn't covered in baby food. Don't overwhelm yourself! Start by taking a bath when you finally get the baby down. Pour some sparkling water into a beautiful wine glass and light a candle. Even if it's for ten minutes, you'll feel so much more relaxed. If you're a single Mom or Dad you're probably thinking you can't even get the kids' toys off the floor! Use your imagination and drop those kids with your neighbors and return the favor when they need a break. If you're just

exhausted by your day, put on some music and dim those lights. But if you're ready now to make some bigger changes, romance your home and yourself by playing the music as loud as you want and painting that room the color that excites you. (Did anyone say platinum entryway?)

No matter what our situations, we can all use an infusion of excitement and glamour from time to time. It might even bring a smile to your face or inspire someone else to get in touch with their sensual side. So go ahead, live on the edge— romance yourself and your home!

CENTS & SENSIBILITY

Add a pair of down throw pillows to your sofa in a gorgeous velvet or silk! If your heart skips a beat when you see them, then you know they're perfect for you.

Drape a luxurious throw of fur, cashmere, mohair, or hand-painted velvet over a not-so-exciting chair or ottoman, and watch it come alive. (Faux fur is fabulous too!)

Collect odd-sized silver or crystal candlesticks. Grouped together, they become more impressive than they ever were alone. Place the group on a mantle or in front of a mirror for double pleasure.

Replace those ordinary white shades your lamps are hiding under; shake things up with something red, black silk with beading, or perforated leather.

Stop treating your windows like they don't matter. Lavish them with the attention they deserve. Spoil yourself with yards of decadent silk and velvet. (But inexpensive fabric works

just as well, as long as you like the look!) Plenty of fabric adds weight and gives the appearance you're trying to achieve. Your windows will know the difference.

Arrange small rounded bouquets of roses (or whatever flowers you prefer!). Place them in unexpected spots for little aromatic sensory surprises. Try the bathroom, bedside, desk, kitchen, and closets.

Play more music—and turn off the TV every now and then. Men may be visual, but women love to be moved by the groove. Find your own favorites.

Select a signature fragrance for your home, as well as for you. Did you know that vanilla is the number one fragrance men are drawn to?

When choosing candles and incense or even aromatic room oils, don't mix scents! Choose one and make the rest the same or scentless. Too much of anything isn't sexy.

Moll

When my husband Charlie and I were waiting for our home to be remodeled, we moved into his old fishing cabin in Dandridge, Tennessee. Charlie was so cute about taking me up there. He was nervous and confessed that he wasn't sure that I was going to be able to handle being an hour's drive away from Knoxville. Truthfully, he feared that the space was a little too rugged and not so elegant for an interior designer like me. Little did he realize that I had lived in smaller quarters than he was taking me; besides, I was a lifestyle saver. I'd earned that title from years of tough times and figuring out how to have more lifestyle for less money. That was my professional training.

It took just 24 hours and a trip to the nearest discount store to turn that rugged space into our hideaway. A fire in the fireplace, some new linens, at least a dozen candles, fresh flowers, some down pillows, a couple of soft throws, and the scent of a home-cooked meal coming from the kitchen. It was a home—our home.

When our house was completed, we packed up everything in the cabin. But before we left, we both ran back in and I took a couple of photos of our very first home together. Charlie and I will never, ever forget it.

THE MAXI MINI

If you're a minimalist, don't despair. You can have your amazing concrete floors and counters and keep that spartan look you know and love, but still add some wow and sparkle. Soften concrete with velvet mohair drapes or furniture. Use throws of luxurious, soft cashmere or a fur that you can drape across a plain bed (and which could also double as an incredible wrap for yourself). Paint a wall lacquer-black for drama or use Venetian plaster with metallics to dazzle. Start small, and ease your way into your new look.

If you're a traditionalist, have no fear! Be bold, and jump into all the classics that you know and love, only add a twist. Instead of hunter green and burgundy, think vivid teals, mesmerizing Mediterranean blues, invigorating oranges, and delicious chocolate browns. For your accessories, punch it up a notch by adding sterling silver and turquoise, pillows of warm leather, or textures with a soft butter feel in sparkling purples or chartreuse. Animal prints are a must as well—just a simple coat or throw pillow in a cheetah print makes a splash and says you might just have an exotic side. If you're fainter of heart, then start with the glamour of breathtaking flowers. Buy a huge vase and go for drama—bigger is always dramatic.

CREATE A RITUAL OF ROMANCE

A friend of mine was struggling a bit in her marriage. She had two small kids, another on the way, and just couldn't seem to find the time for herself or her relationship. One night we decided that what she needed was a nightly ritual so that she could unwind at the end of each day. She started a routine where every night she and her husband would put the toys away and clean the dishes together before putting the kids to bed. Then when they came back down stairs, the space was once again "adult space." They would just sit, talk, and spend time together. Sometimes it was just ten minutes, other times an hour; either way, it was time spent in a relaxing atmosphere to recharge themselves.

Create a ritual of escape for yourself. It doesn't have to just be for you and a romantic partner. What sort of environment recharges you? Think about using all of your senses. If you could, what would you do every day to "escape"—even if just for ten minutes. Let yourself be romanced by your home.

Moll Anderson client

Come to your senses

Name a movie or piece of art that stimulates your senses. What is it about this visual experience that gets to you? (Color, texture, imagery?)

_____

_____

_____

_____

_____

_____

_____

_____

_____

_____

What is the least attractive space in your home? Why? Name three things that you learned in this chapter that can help you connect to your senses in that room.

_____

_____

_____

_____

_____

_____

_____

_____

_____

Write a love poem to yourself from the perspective of your home. Why do you and your home deserve to be romanced?

Create a list of things you find sensual. Name a food, a song, a color, a fabric, a beverage, a movie, a book, a country, a language, a person, a time of day, an item from nature, a name—the list can go on and on. Start there and see what you come up with.

How do you paint yourself out of a corner? Pick up a paintbrush! It's a great way to get your energy flowing and add a little living color into a life that may sometimes seem a bit drab. Paint not only is one of the most affordable decorating tools we have, but can quickly elevate your mood! And with the power to add just the right punch of excitement, romance, or energy you seek, paint is not just about color anymore! Painting techniques can bring the texture and depth to a room you need to bring some life back into your lifestyle. So add a splash of wow to your home—and roll away those blues!

PAINT
yourself out of a corner™

PAINT
yourself out of a corner

When you physically and mentally decide to make a change, keep it simple—start with color. Becoming physically motivated to paint is an incredible stress-buster that makes you more open and susceptible to the possibility of change. When we become restless or lethargic and we don't know what's wrong, we're sometimes afraid to face the reality of our situations. Sometimes we become static, and other times we go nuts and act out! So try a little paint to roll away the mental cobwebs, and add a little sunshine to your life.

What colors naturally draw you? Are you more attracted to deep earth tones? Or light, airy hues? Color—a marvelous form of energy—has an amazing impact on the human psyche. I won't get into the physics of it, but just know that each color has an energy specific to it. When you look at a rainbow, you see the colors red through violet with the range of all the colors in between. This spectrum goes from the highest energy (red) to the lowest energy (violet). Red isn't just *perceived* to be more energetic, it actually *is!* So when choosing a color, consider the energy it gives off.

Let go of the belief that the past could have been any different.

—GARY ZUKAV

72

Start by deciding what it is you're missing and what you're feeling about yourself, your relationships, and your life in general. If you've been depressed or feel stuck, try a color that is invigorating and full of energy like orange—or at least a tone in the same family, such as pumpkin.

If you're looking to spice up your love life and want to try something new in the boudoir, choose one of the many exotic, jeweled tones like reds and plums. Reds add passion and symbolize courage. Sensual and luxurious, the regal plums and purples help you feel like royalty. The bedroom is a great place to be a little more daring, so go for it!

But maybe you seek more light and peace in your home. Consider those hues that match the colors of the Mediterranean. Tranquil and serene blues attract people who tend to be calm and very cool. Or perhaps you love the clean, fresh crispness of white! Just remember: The white you think you love may not actually be plain white; white offers many shades. I suggest a warmer tone of white—it's more universally flattering.

Whatever ails you, there's a color to help chase away the blues. If you're stressed from work, try something soothing like muted steel. Or if you're having a hard time getting motivated to make a change, take a chance with something vibrant—a deep orange-red or raspberry. Most important, don't be afraid of color or of making a mistake in choosing color. Live dangerously and dare to pick a color no one would ever believe you'd choose, or at least one that will affect you and your home in a new and interesting way. After all, it's only paint. But I promise you that you'll get more mileage out of it than any other decorating tool.

So instead of living in that rut, paint yourself out of it!

Painting is an attempt to come to terms with life. There are as many solutions as there are human beings. —GEORGE TOOKER

Moll

My client Jan moved out of her boyfriend's house because the relationship was heading anywhere but marriage. She had the guts to get out, stand on her own two feet, and remain open to the possibility of a future relationship with someone who wanted the same things she wanted. It was a tough decision to leave someone she loved, but ultimately she had no choice.

Jan rented a great little apartment, and we had a long talk over pizza the first night she moved in. Because this apartment was only temporary ("I'll be here only six months or so"), she told me she wouldn't spend any money fixing it up. "Besides," she said, "it's not really mine." That was almost ten years ago! I visited recently and half-jokingly suggested just painting the entryway, "We can paint it that fabulous raspberry color you've been talking about all these years." But Jan wouldn't go for it. She insisted this was the year she would be moving into her real place.

Jan has never really quite made that apartment her home, even though she's still living in it. It wouldn't take much, just a little paint and some elbow grease. Action is a fabulous motivator.

Before

After

What better way to add some kick to your space than with a warm palette of spice-inspired hues? The colors of chili powder, red pepper, paprika, and cayenne are sure to add some heat to your home. Red is an emotionally intense hue that even has physical effects; it can enhance metabolism, increase respiration, and raise blood pressure! It is most typically associated with passion, desire, and love; however, energy, power, and determination are also closely connected with this color. A reddish-brown tone is associated with harvest and fall and is a great way to bring in a sense of the natural world without going neutral. Get inspired by an autumn walk through your imagination and paint your walls the fall leaf colors of sugar maple, sassafras, or scarlet oak. Whatever your inspiration, a warm palette filled with reds and deep browns is sure to evoke a sense both of comfort and passion in the same stroke.

Remember when you were young and it seemed completely possible that you could live on a cloud? Well, a soft, soothing palette of muted blues and cottony whites is just about as close as you can get. Blue, so closely associated with the earth elements of sky and water, communicates depth and stability. A symbol of honesty, integrity, confidence, wisdom, faith, and Heaven, blue is said to soothe the mind and body. It slows metabolism and calms the psyche. The combination of pale blue and white can often come across as nursery-like unless paired with something earthy. So highlight its association with tranquility and purity by bringing in rich neutrals like chocolate brown and steel gray. The opposite of red and orange on a color wheel, blue suppresses the appetite; so consider blue for a bedroom rather than the kitchen!

THE FINISH LINE

After color, paint finish is next in terms of importance. The finish is the amount of light that is reflected off the surface once the paint has dried. The range of finishes goes from flat (little or no light reflected) to high gloss (a glossy sheen where a significant amount of light is reflected).

Flat paint, sometimes called **matte**, is most often used for interior walls. Since it doesn't reflect a lot of light, it does a good job of hiding minor imperfections on the surface of the wall. Don't, however, feel that just because it's usually done that way, you have to use flat paint for your interior walls. A high-gloss or semigloss sheen on an accent wall in your bedroom could make quite a statement!

A **satin** finish, sometimes referred to as **eggshell**, is the next step up in terms of sheen. If you don't like the sometimes-chalky look of matte paint, try an eggshell finish to give it a creamy, buttery look.

A **semigloss** finish may be a good choice for a humid room, such as a bathroom or basement rec-room, due to its ability to repel moisture. Sometimes the walls of a bathroom can mildew if it's not properly protected. But if you like the look of flat paint rather than a semigloss finish, there are mildew-inhibiting products available that you can use to prime your walls before you apply your favorite matte color!

Last, but definitely not least, is **high gloss**! High gloss is most commonly used for trim and painting furniture. Along with being a great moisture repellent, a higher gloss finish is easier to maintain. One reason it's often used for trim (besides the fact that it can catch the light off of some fabulous crown molding) is that it doesn't stain or show dirty fingerprints as much as a flat paint would. Just think about how much more often a cabinet or a doorframe is touched compared to the wall behind a sofa!

Thus, the finish isn't purely for looks; it serves a functional purpose too! Remember: Finishes go from dull to glossy. The higher the gloss, the more durable it is. But keep in mind that even though it's easier to maintain, it might not look like it because it can highlight the imperfections of the wall itself. Many paint companies have recently developed "washable" flat paints that clean like a semigloss but hide like a flat.

What Is Latex, Anyway?

Latex is just a fancy word for water-based paint. Most home-interior paints are latex due to their easy cleanup, faster dry-time, and lower fume emissions. Oil-based paints still have their place in high-shine jobs. Oil-based paints take longer to dry, and they can cause quite the fume overload at times, but if you have the time (and the brain cells to spare), cabinets finished in a high-gloss oil paint can be stunning. In the end, it really comes down to preference and the specific job, so don't be overwhelmed by the oil vs. latex debate.

Just remember that if you're using oil-based paint, you have to use mineral spirits for cleanup. Water won't do the trick. The odor of mineral spirits can be rather overpowering, though, so try an odorless brand!

Go Green

These days, people increasingly seek environmentally friendly products. Paint is now available that is less hazardous to your indoor air quality! Look for paints with low VOC (volatile organic compound) and low odor ratings to do yourself and your home a favor!

Walking through Hong Kong could have been the inspiration for this striking room. The old Chinese pottery was perhaps plucked right off a small antique shop shelf as you ducked into a quiet corner, away from the hustle of traffic in the street. There it was, regal and sophisticated, sitting pretty and all by itself. In that moment, you wanted to carry that feeling back to your own quiet place to accent and inspire your home. Your classic creamy white room is the perfect place to inspire this vibe with colors drawn from your new find. One reason navy has stood the test of time is that dark blue represents depth, seriousness, and dependability—talk about having qualities with staying power! Starting with a neutral palette is a great way to keep your ever-changing look versatile. Bring life to this basic canvas with bold accents that represent your inspirational whims—no matter what they are! Travel through your mind and heart and try to capture the vibe that you want your room to communicate to you every single day.

A neutral palette doesn't have to be boring. Whether it's alabaster, downy, cream, ivory, beige, or ecru, there isn't just one "white." Use whites with warm, golden undertones. It complements most hues and gives off a warm glow—consider it the candle of colors! As shades of warm white become darker, you start to move into the wheat and gold hues. Gold denotes illumination, wisdom, and wealth, and often symbolizes high quality and evokes feelings of prestige. Mixing golden hues with earthy whites is a great way to evoke this sense of "prestige" in a more natural and understated manner. A soft neutral palette such as this is also the perfect place to experiment with rich textures. Try metallic touches, rustic woods, sheer linens, and bold details like fringe. Since the colors won't be competing for attention, give your room some interest with things to touch and feel.

READY SET GO!

Once again, the list of items you "need" in order to paint may seem to go on and on, but you *really* need only a few simple ones.

Brush-up

You use a brush to paint furniture, trim, and the area of the wall next to the trim (a process called "cutting-in"). I recommend an angled brush to give you more control while cutting-in at the baseboards and in the corners. It gives a cleaner line than the regular flat-head brush.

On a Roll

All rollers are basically the same. It's the roller cover that varies just a bit. I recommend using a poly-wool blend cover because it can be used with both oil and latex paints. Natural covers such as mohair or sheepskin are ideal when using high-gloss, oil-based paint in order to give a smooth lint-free finish. A variety of specialty covers are available for different metallic or textured finishes.

Tip: When painting a wall with a roller, cross over your strokes to cover more evenly, rather than painting in perfect vertical rows.

Tray-ning Day

It's really your choice what type tray (metal or plastic) you'd rather use. Plastic is generally less expensive and works just the same. But make sure you get a sturdy plastic tray, not just a flimsy liner. If you try to move the flimsy tray when it's full of paint, you'll end up with a dirty drop cloth, rather than dramatic walls.

Under Cover

When it comes to painting, one of the most essential items is a drop cloth! Yes, you can paint the walls without one, but can you really enjoy the color if it's all over the floors, too?

Tip: Even though you have a drop cloth, still take some care. Large spills can sometimes seep through, so get a cloth that's at least 1mm thick. Also, check your feet before you walk into the kitchen to take a water break. I paint in socks and then have a pair of slippers or flip-flops by the doorway to change into before I leave the room! That way I protect my pedicure, shoes, and floors.

Prime Time

Primer can be a painter's best friend. Why waste an extra gallon of expensive high-gloss paint to cover the red wall beneath if you can use just one coat of primer instead? Primers are fantastic because they can be tinted to make your job easier. For example, say that you have a pale yellow wall that you want to paint a deep scarlet. Your local paint store can tint the primer with a bit of red. Primer can also solve issues such as mildew or stains. You'll find several great stain-blocking, mildew-fighting, and fungus-busting primers out there. Priming the wall may seem like an extra step, but it saves you a lot of time in the long run!

Keep in mind that if you're using a latex-based paint, you'll need a latex-based primer. The same goes for oil-based paint—you'll need an oil-based primer.

Adding a twist of lemon or lime to any drink is quite the refresher. Well, the same goes for this citrus-inspired palette. That added bit of zest is sometimes just what your room calls for. I'm sure some of you are turned off by the thought of a lime-green room, but keep in mind that just because your inspiration is a fresh bowl of citrus doesn't mean that you have to use that hue directly. Tone down a key-lime color for a more modern look, or pair citrus colors with deep browns for a contemporary feel. Due to their close association with the fruits, citrus hues are linked with health and vitality. They arouse feelings of warmth, promote cheer, and encourage mental activity. So freshen up your family room with muted hues of lemon-lime, and add a twist to your style.

PAINT
yourself out of a corner

Bring home a bit of balmy atmosphere from your last tropical vacation, or simply give yourself the getaway you deserve right in your own home! Crank up the heat with this lush, island-inspired palette, and get lost doing the limbo in your living room. This vibrant combo, inspired by your favorite exotic locale, is full of passion, yet still manages a bit of understated elegance. Complement it with dark hardwoods and rich exotic textures. If this palette seems active to you, that's because it is! Orange has a physical effect of increasing oxygen supply to the brain, evoking a rush of mental activity and stimulating the appetite. Interestingly, orange is a highly accepted color among youth. So whether you're looking to bring the islands back with you or just to get away for a while, pick a palette that takes cues from Cuba (or any tropical locale), and feel the temperature rise.

REAL OR FAUXBULOUS?

You've got the basics down; now you just want a few ideas to take it from average to amazing. Here are some suggestions to really add some drama to your style.

Heavy Metal

Innately royal and luxurious, metallics immediately boost the atmosphere. I recently painted my office bathroom a metallic bronze. It increased the wow factor in that tiny space tenfold! Metallics are also a great way to highlight furniture with great lines. Think Louis XIV with a contemporary twist! Try adding silver leaf to a ceiling (it can be costly, so start small), or gold leaf to the feet of a chair. Metallic spray paint on small accessories can make quite a statement!

In a Glaze of Glory

A great way to add depth and character to an otherwise plain wall or piece of furniture, glazes, just like paint, come in a variety of colors and finishes. But glaze is just a transparent—"watered down"—version. If you want to age a white chest, consider using an ochre or tobacco glaze in a matte finish to wash over it. Don't worry about being perfect. The more imperfect the better—it will look more natural. Another high-drama glazing technique is to use a high-gloss glaze over an otherwise average wall. Since the glaze is transparent, you can't really go wrong with the color selection; just pick something you like. Glaze kicks it up a notch! Don't worry if the glaze drips a bit and pools in the natural creases of the wall or furniture. Such imperfections make your piece unique and interesting!

Faux finishes by Deb Staver of DEB STAVER DESIGNS

Brush It Off

Think beyond the brush and the roller. Paint can be applied in a variety of ways to add a unique, artistic quality to your walls. Sponging, ragging, and dragging are just a few techniques. You might also try using plastic bags and spatulas to apply paint to your walls! The possibilities are endless.

Don't Faux Yourself Into a Corner

Sometimes when you're looking at the faux technique used on a whole room or wall, it's very obvious where people started and where they stopped. So be sure to start in the center of the wall and work your way out in a circular fashion. If you have a painting partner, try switching from side-to-side so it's not so obvious whose side is whose. Delineation between your side and your partner's is a not-so-fauxbulous result. Also, remember that you can't really mess up. If you don't like the way it looks, dampen a rag with some water (mineral spirits if the paint is oil-based) and just wipe it down. It might not be exactly the look you were expecting—it might be better!

Want to feel rejuvenated? Create a spa-like retreat using a palette of soothing, natural hues. Green, always aligned with nature, symbolizes freshness, growth, and fertility. It is believed to have healing power. As the most restful color for the human eye, it can even improve vision! Take a cue from a walk in the forest, and pair mossy hues with other earthy tones like stone, slate, and putty. Basic brown, the other quintessential color of nature, signifies stability and is the perfect way to get in touch with your senses. Whether it's a bathroom, a living room, a bedroom, or a kitchen, pull your palette from natural elements and create an inviting place to escape from the day. Enhance the feelings of relaxation and escape by including other lifestyle elements such as scented candles and plush, comfortable fabrics.

The ultimate power palette, black and metallics are a sleek solution for any space. This combo is certain to add an element of distinction and formality to any home environment. Black may sometimes be seen as a "negative" hue, but nine times out of ten, the driver of a black car is either successful—or on her way to being successful! So use black to your advantage and let it inspire you to success. Bring it into your home using luxurious leathers and high-gloss finishes. Pair it with sophisticated touches like stainless steel fixtures and faux-fur throws. Get inspired by a slab of polished marble—or your favorite eyeliner! Whether it's ebony, charcoal, or gun-metal gray, black is back and better than ever. Glam it up with metallics, crisp it up with white, or brighten it up with (almost) any hue. Be bold with black, and see where it takes you.

SADDLE UP!

Like the look of leather? Here is a technique that uses glaze and plastic drop cloths to achieve this luxuriously textured finish.

> ## Shopping List
> **Standard roller**
> **2 poly-blend roller covers**
> **Semigloss latex paint** (base coat)
> **Glaze** (top coat)
> **Several 1mm thick plastic drop cloths**
> (the number needed depends on the size of the room)

Faux Leather

Venetian Plaster

1 Paint on your semigloss basecoat, and allow it to dry.

2 Roll the glaze onto the wall in manageable sections. (Manageable means that you do *not* want the glaze to dry before you move to the next step!)

3 Press one of the 1mm thick plastic drop cloths to the wall. The glaze will help the plastic sheet stick to the wall's surface.

4 "Smoosh" the plastic over the wet glaze. Allow the plastic to wrinkle.

5 Peel the plastic off the glaze while the glaze is still wet; discard the plastic.

6 Move to the next section and repeat steps 2 to 5. Overlap the areas of wet glaze to avoid distinctive marks between the sections.

The Finish Line
Once all the sections are complete, you will be left with a crinkled glaze effect that has the look of leather, minus the cost and animal cruelty.

GET PLASTERED

One of my favorite faux finishes is Venetian plaster. Although the process can be quite labor intensive, the results are spectacular! Venetian plaster is a multi-step process, so read through all the directions before you start.

> ## Shopping List
> **Venetian plaster compound**
> **A smooth steel trowel*** (rounded edges & no teeth)
> **Sandpaper** (400 or 600 grit)

Compound Coat #1

1. Load your well-mixed plaster compound onto the steel trowel.

2. Holding the trowel at a 15- to 30-degree angle to the wall, start in a corner and apply the plaster in short, patchy strokes.

3. Spread the compound thinly on the wall, alternating both short and long strokes. There is no need to spread the plaster perfectly; in this coat, you want some of the wall surface below to show through. Wipe off the trowel as you go to avoid leaving ridges and bits of dried plaster as you spread.

4. Allow this coat of plaster to dry thoroughly (approximately 4 hours).

Compound Coat # 2

1. Load the trowel with the Venetian plaster compound and start in the same corner.

2. Apply the compound in alternating short and long strokes just as before; however, this time, hold the trowel at a 60- to 90-degree angle to the wall and overlap your strokes.

3. Again, spread the plaster using varying strokes of short and long; however, this time, fill in any recesses and exposed areas of the wall.

4. Use the trowel to smooth away any unwanted edge marks that the trowel may have left behind.

5. Allow this coat of plaster to dry for approximately 24 hours.

The Finish Line

Using either 400 or 600 grit sandpaper, rub over the entire surface until the desired degree of shine is achieved. For large areas, save time and sweat by using a power sander.

Rub a damp rag over the entire wall surface to remove the plaster dust that was created during sanding.

*(*Note: If you cannot find a metal trowel with rounded edges, you can round it off yourself. Use either 100 grit sandpaper or a file to round the edges, and follow it up with a finer grit sandpaper.)*

PROJECT

Though often considered the province of only the wealthy or connoisseurs, art is for anyone! In fact, the best part of art is that it is subjective. It's about what *you* like, what evokes your emotion, what sparks your inspiration. So why don't you create your own art?

Sure, it may seem a little scary, but it's a lot easier than you might think. You never know what you'll come up with, and at the very least, you'll have fun doing it! It's also a great way to experiment with color—without committing to painting an entire room.

Canvas

Buy prepared canvas from your local art or craft store. Gallery-wrapped canvases have no staples on the sides—thus, you won't have to frame them! Canvases come in a range of sizes, but I always say, the bigger the better. You can get canvases in a variety of thicknesses ($1/2$ to 3 inches). The $1\,1/2$ - and 3-inch thicknesses are my favorites because they look professional—no matter what is on them!

Paint

Get cheap acrylic paint; there's no need to break the bank! Just get large tubes of the least expensive paint you can find in your favorite colors.

Media

You can use a variety of media to add texture and depth to your work. For example, you'll find some great sand, stucco, and gloss additives, but those products can get expensive. Torn paper, playground sand, or water washes can give equally interesting effects.

Brushes

Brushes come in many sizes—and prices. For this sort of project, there's no reason to spend a ton of money on brushes. Many art and craft stores sell packages that include several brushes in a variety of sizes. Large brushes make your job easier in the end! A 3- or 4-inch brush can make some really expressive strokes. Get one at your local home-improvement or hardware store. (You might even have one around the house from painting your walls!)

Sponges

Sponges are another great way to apply paint to canvas. Use anything from textured sea sponges to a kitchen sponge (you might want to start with a fresh one, though). Sponges provide a variety of textures, from rough and stippled to smooth and blended.

SHOPPING LIST

Canvas

Paint

Media

Brushes

Sponges

Palette

Drop Cloth

Palette

Disposable painter's palettes are great, but you could also use plastic plates or wax paper taped over a piece of cardboard. Use something disposable for easy clean-up, but if you'd rather not create waste, use a piece of thick plastic or glass—just tape off the edges if the surfaces are sharp!

Drop Cloth

You can't let loose if you worry about making a mess. Cover the floor with a drop cloth, or paint outside! Even though acrylic paint is water-

Water

The greatest thing about acrylic paint (besides being affordable) is that it is water-based! This means that it can be thinned out and cleaned up using just water. You'll need a bowl or tray of water to wash your brush and thin out the paint. When you're done, wash out your brush using mild soap and warm water until the water runs clear.

based and can usually be cleaned using warm water and mild soap on solid surfaces, it's a tad trickier on fabric and carpeting. Wear a smock or clothes you don't care about getting a little color on.

Inspiration

Look for what inspires you—an image from a book, a color scheme in a photograph, or a part of the landscape. Art is your interpretation of what inspires you. Don't worry about copying something exactly; you're painting, not taking a photograph!

JUST DO IT!

You've got your supplies, the drop cloth is down, and now you're just staring at a big, very white, blank canvas. It's intimidating! Even "real artists" are intimidated by a blank canvas. The only way to get over that is to paint.

You might look at the works of famous (or not-so-famous) artists to get an idea about what sort of art you like best. Within the field of abstract art, there are three major movements: Neoplasticism, Cubism, and Abstract Expressionism. I'm not here to give you an art history lesson, but you may find inspiration in these artistic revolutions!

For me, the easiest movement to get started with, and the one most aligned with this project, is Abstract Expressionism. This division of Abstract Art is about expressing emotion and movement through texture, stroke, and color. Abstract Expressionism is divided into two movements, Action Painting and Color Field Painting. Jackson Pollock is one of the best-

Every artist was first an amateur.

—RALPH WALDO EMERSON

known action painters. Pollock would lay the canvas on the ground on the ground and splatter layers and layers of paint onto the surface until the paint built up a web of texture and color. Action Painting is meant to show the action of both the paint and the artist (hence its name!).

Color Field Painting is best represented by Mark Rothko. It is the study of how large blocks of colors interact with one another when placed together on the canvas. Rothko's paintings often look like large abstract landscapes. Choose colors from your inspiration (or from the palettes in this section) and paint two-thirds of the canvas with one color and the other third with another. Paint that drips between the color

blocks is great. If you don't like the color combinations, keep going! A little bit of another color peeking through adds interest. Also, try adding pieces of paper or enlarged photographs. The acrylic paint will usually adhere the paper to the canvas (but white glue works as well).

This is *your* art, *your* inspiration, and *your* interpretation of the world. Take a look at the work of artists but don't get caught up in trying to reproduce what they have done. Let your energy and passions loose in a productive and artistic manner!

Just remember:

- Imperfection in art is what makes it interesting.
- If you make a "mistake," you can always change it (but usually it's the "mistakes" that make the art).
- This is going to be fun!

Let It Move You

1) Turn on some music that fits the mood of what you want to paint. Do you want something with a lot of energy, or perhaps something a bit more mellow? Tune out the rest of the world

(distractions, daily stresses, your fears, everything else), and lose yourself in the moment. Art is an experience, not an outcome.

2) Prepare your palette, or just squeeze paint directly on the canvas! The nice thing about using a palette is that you can mix the colors so you're not only using colors directly from the tube.
Tip: Think about your inspiration. Let it move you. What colors are you attracted to? Which shapes? Do you like large blocks of color or swirling lines? Smooth surfaces or textured ones?

3) Prep your canvas. Giving your canvas a wash of color gets rid of the stark, ready-made canvas look, as well as create a homogenized background. In a small bowl, mix water and paint. The water thins the paint enough to make this process easier and give a washed effect to the canvas. I love prepping my canvases with anything from chocolate brown to deep teal or rusty red—it's really up to you!
Tip: Be daring! Just because the color palette you've chosen is mostly blues and greens doesn't mean that you can't have a deep pumpkin background. The contrast between the colors has a lot of energy and movement! Experiment.

4) Enlarge photographs or phrases! You can add paper to create texture and interest. How about adding a family photograph or your favorite quote? Enlarge the image as much as you want at a copy center; I love when the image starts to get grainy and a bit distorted—remember, imperfection is perfection. Try tearing the edges of the paper, or including only a portion of the original image. Attach the paper using white glue, and add layers of paint and glaze over the image to really incorporate it into the canvas!

Fabric is not just for the furniture! Consider adding leftover remnants of lace or pieces of an old shirt to your painting. Attach them to the canvas the same way you would a piece of paper.

5) Once you're done, let your painting dry and enjoy. You're now on your way to an amazing original art collection!
Tip: Who's to say that "done" means forever? If you ever feel the desire to change your piece of art, take it off the wall and add to it. I've been known to repaint my art whenever I update a room. Sometimes I just add a slash of the color I've introduced into the space.

What is the color of your parachute?

Look at the color palettes on the previous pages. What do they mean to you? Write the first three words or phrases that come to mind when you look at each. They can be an adjective, a person, a place, a song, a food, a memory—anything.

From the palettes, choose the ones that most attract you. Do the descriptions match your personality? Assign color palettes to your family and friends too!

Think of a happy memory. What colors stand out to you? Can you visualize them?

Or do you get more of a feeling? Can you translate that feeling into a color?

Assign a color to each room in your home based on the feelings you want to evoke in each space.

Use the palette descriptions as well as your own personal associations.

Is there a room in your home that needs as much of an emotional facelift as an aesthetic one?

Discuss the emotional connection that you have to that room, and why you'd like to change it.

A flip of the switch or the strike of a match changes the mood of the room. But more than that, mood *lighting* is a natural phenomenon. An overcast day, a romantic sunset, or a brilliant, mysterious full moon—lighting affects us on a primal level. We are innately programmed to be moved by light. So why not use this easy (and inexpensive) tool to alter the ambiance of the place where you live? Try these great tips to light up your home (and brighten your day).

LIGHT *dim and dimmer*

unrise, sunset, rainbows, and lightning. Think about how these beautiful natural phenomena make you feel. A bright day energizes many of us. Some become moody when the sky is overcast and gray; for others, the sunset creates tranquility. Doctors even use light therapy to treat patients. So why wouldn't we use the dramatic effects of light to our advantage in our homes? It's the quickest way to change the personality of a room.

We have grown up in a culture addicted to the sun. Sunlight feels so good; its warmth signifies comfort and health. It's only natural we want to bring light into our homes.

To begin with, make sure each room in your house has several light sources. As much as light is about "mood," keep its practical reasons in mind, as well. Nothing is more frustrating than trying to put your make-up on in a dark bathroom or straining to see what color suit you have on so you can match your socks. Match the lighting to your needs.

Natural light is ideal for most tasks. You can do everything under the sun (pun intended) with natural light—not to mention you'll save money on your electric bill! If your home doesn't have a lot of sources for natural light, a few simple changes can still give your home a more naturally lit look. The idea is to fill your space with light.

While special lamps are available that duplicate the look of natural light, they can be costly. Nice overhead lights (*not* fluorescents) work well. After all, natural light comes from above, so we tend to view overhead lighting as the "real deal." If overheads aren't an option, try placing several lamps around the room to help fill the space with light.

Bulbs give off either a blue light or a yellow light. Blue is crisper and "more natural," while yellow light is warmer and more soothing. Go with the color you prefer. Either way, don't fight (or ignore) the fact that you don't have tons of natural light; go out and buy some!—and when you do, think *ambiance*.

Direct light is best suited for specific tasks such as reading or sewing. Task lights do the job and don't take up much space. Generally, direct light is too harsh for everyday use, so avoid it unless the task requires it. After all, who wants to live under a spotlight? Unless, of course, you have a piece of art or furniture that you want to show off. Even an inexpensive piece of art—something self-made or a framed print—can become dramatic when highlighted by a small picture light.

Speaking of art, you'll find lamps so cool today that they can be considered an architectural piece. Not only do lamps come in all shapes and sizes, but most lamp shops can take just about anything and turn it into a lamp. Jars, bowling balls, driftwood—if you can think of it, they can make it.

Lampshades, too, add pizzazz to a room (and can easily update a tired lamp). You'll find all kinds of colors and sizes. For a particularly striking effect, look for shades lined with gold. Lovely and luminous, they cast a warm glow around the room.

One of the best investments you can make to alter your atmosphere is a dimmer switch. Inexpensive and really simple to install, they soften the lights instantly, adding drama and intimacy to a room. I also love to incorporate

In the right light, at the right time,
everything is extraordinary.

—AARON ROSE

soft-pink bulbs, which produce a wonderful, relaxing light that's perfect for unwinding at home after a long fluorescent-filled day at the office. Softer light flatters the skin and adds rich tones to your room.

Of course, candles are always a terrific way to set a mood. Get creative by using a variety of sizes, colors, and scents. The mood of a room—and perhaps your day—can shift when you just light some candles. The subtle flickering light creates a tranquil atmosphere. But choose your scents carefully. Just as you must consider dueling aromas when preparing a meal (a filet mignon topped with caramel fudge doesn't sound so appetizing, does it?), select candle scents that blend well to produce a mood that soothes, not sickens. Or select candles that have no scent; beeswax is perfect.

Another lighting consideration is camouflage. If your paint and fabric aren't quite worth showcasing, just dim the lights. Let mood take center stage over the old worn arm of the sofa. Everything looks better when lit properly for effect.

So the next time you need a quick, easy way to add ambiance, think lighting. The flick of a switch or the strike of a match can turn your home from bland to brilliant!

COMMON SCENTS

Candles can play double duty in the ambiance department. Not only do they provide the obvious sense soother (soft lighting), but they also come in a variety of scents that soothe your other senses, as well. No matter what mood you'd like to present, there's a scent to set the stage.

For This Mood	Try These Scents
Relaxing	Chamomile, Thyme, French Lavender
Sensual	Clove, Musk, Merlot, Fig, Tuberose, Honey
Revitalizing	Pomegranate-Citrus, Peppermint, Tangerine
Fresh	Cucumber-Mint, Linen, Cranberry, Lime-Basil
Tropical	Pineapple-Ginger, Bamboo-Hibiscus, Coconut
Inviting	Cappuccino-Nutmeg, Pumpkin, Rhubarb-Vanilla

Have you ever heard the phrase "too much of a good thing?" Well, this definitely applies to candle scents. Just because you like the smell of mango and cappuccino separately doesn't mean that the combo will double the pleasure. When purchasing your candles, hold the combination of scents you are considering together and take a whiff of the collective aroma, rather than smelling each separately. That way your nose won't have a rude awakening once you burn them in the same space.

A COORDINATED EFFORT

The color of a candle often coordinates with its scent. Sometimes this leaves you with a great smelling room and fantastic lighting, but what happens when the candles aren't lit, and you're left with an accessory that just doesn't color coordinate? There are a few options to fix this problem: You can purchase brands of candles that come in only one, neutral color no matter what the scent. Place the candles into cool votives or a unique holder. Or you can make your own candle with a DIY (Do It Yourself) kit; that way you pick both the color and scent to suit your needs.

There are two kinds of light—the glow that illuminates, and the glare that obscures.

—JAMES THURBER

FLAME WORTHY

- When lighting candles, trim the wick to ¼ inch before lighting. That way, you avoid a smoky carbon build-up from your burning candle.

- Candles are pretty, fire trucks are not. Just use your head and be careful. If you have kids, speak to them about fire safety. Always extinguish every candle before leaving the house or going to sleep.

- If you love the ambiance of dripping candles, then get savvy to the trick of wax cleanup. All you need is a very hot iron and a grocery store brown paper bag. Lay the paper bag directly on the fabric or carpet where the wax has spilt, and place the hot iron on the bag. The wax will melt into the paper bag. This trick has saved my floors and linens from many drip-filled nights.

- Burning dripless candles can solve the drip dilemma.

- Candles can transfer a black, sooty residue onto your walls if burned too close to a surface or for long periods. If you do have a wall that seems to have some carbon build-up, and scrubbing it hasn't done the trick, then keep a can of touch-up paint stored away to paint over the worn sections.

Life is not just boring black and white. Its interest comes from the gray area that we live in every day. The same goes for lighting. Dimmer switches are a simple solution to add a little middle ground between off and on, and bring life to your lighting.

Dimmer switches come in four popular varieties: slide, dial, touchpad, and switch/slide combo. Read the directions for your particular device.

But this easy step-by-step installation process takes almost no time and will work with any dimmer type.

Safety First: Be sure that the power to the circuit you are working on is turned off at the main breaker box or fuse panel. Breakers: Find the right breaker in the breaker box, and flip it to the "Off" position. Fuses: If you have a fuse box, find the right fuse and remove it completely from the panel. Test that the power to the circuit has been disconnected by simply flipping the switch to the "On" position and confirming the lights remain off. (Once the switch plate is removed, you can double-check that the circuit is disconnected by testing the wires with a circuit tester if you wish.)

1 Use a screwdriver or reversible cordless drill with a screwdriver attachment to remove the existing switch plate.

2 Remove the switch from the exposed workbox by unscrewing the screws at the bottom of the switch. (This is the step where you can double-check that the circuit is off using a circuit tester.)

3 Disconnect the wires that are attached to the light switch. There should be three wires: black, white, and green (it may be a bare copper wire in some cases).

4 Use the wire cutters to cut the three exposed wires just below their plastic coverings. Strip the wire to about 3/8 inch using the wire cutters or a wire stripper (this tool makes the job of stripping much easier, but isn't necessary).

5 Connect the black wire in the existing box to the black wire on the new dimmer switch by placing the two exposed wires next to each other and twisting on a wire nut (make sure that the bare wire is completely encased in the wire nut). Repeat for the white wires and the ground wires (green or brass), as well.

6 Bend the wires in a zigzag pattern so that they easily fit back into the workbox. Push the switch into place, and adjust it so that it is straight and so that the orientation of the switch is correct (up is "On" and down is "Off," for instance). Tighten the two screws to hold it in position.

7 Install the new switch plate by tightening the provided plate screws.

8 Switch the breaker box back on, or reinstall the fuse.

9 Test your new dimmer switch to make sure the installation was a success—and enjoy!
(If the switch does not work, turn off your breaker or fuse again, and double-check your wiring. Check that black is with black, white is with white, and so on. Also be sure that the wire nuts are tight and secure.)

SHOPPING LIST

Dimmer switch kit

Screwdriver

Wire cutters

Cordless drill & screwdriver attachment

Needle-nose pliers

Circuit tester

I put dimmer switches in every room possible, even the laundry room. That room often becomes a coatroom for parties when I put a collapsible clothes rack there. The first time I transformed the laundry to a coatroom, I ended up putting a lamp on top of the dryer so the room would have the right ambiance for my party. It worked—but the next day I installed a dimmer in the laundry room!

— Moll

STAINED GLASS LANTERNS

Turn glass lanterns into stained glass. It's easy to create fabulous decorative lighting for indoors or out using clear glass lanterns and stained glass paint. Make several to hang in a tree outside or set in a group on a dining table.

Shopping List

Glass lanterns (must be clear but can have etching)
Candles (to fit lanterns)
Stained glass paint (from a craft supply store)
Brushes (an assortment of sizes up to an inch wide)
Thin painter's tape (as thin as possible)

Use the painter's tape to mark out the borders of your design. You can be as simple or as complex as you wish—standard stripes to intricate swirls and everything in between. (You can paint on the glass freehand without the tape, but the tape gives the finished product a crisper look.) Using the stained glass paint and a brush, apply your colors of choice. Let dry and enjoy!

BASKET CASE

Think outside the box, and turn unusual items into lighting fixtures. You can transform virtually any object into a lamp. Whether you buy a lamp-making kit, employ the assistance of your local lamp store, or use the simple method described below, you can take anything from an antique vase to an old fruit crate and turn in into a luminary masterpiece. It's so easy—so get creative!

For example, here's what you can do with a rattan wastebasket:
1. Get a rattan wastebasket with no metal base.
2. Purchase a contractor light from your local home-improvement center.
3. Remove the clamp and the can from the light.
4. Punch through the bottom of the basket to make a hole just big enough to pull lighting cord through. (A screwdriver or sharp knife will work. If not, you can always drill a hole that's the appropriate size.)
5. Turn the wastebasket upside down, and pull the cord through the hole, covering the cord with a chandelier cord cover.
6. Hang it up, and plug it in!

That's it, and now you have a one-of-a-kind lighting fixture!

Moll

It was Milan, Italy, and I was on tour, singing with a pop/rock group—a wonderful, once-in-a-lifetime experience. Our group consisted of me and two amazingly talented people with whom I've been friends ever since, Paula Nichols Keane and Joe Milner. We were waiting to hook up with our producer and the label the following day. Because of the Easter holiday, we couldn't get our per diem, so we were broke. Fortunately, Paula spoke Italian, Joe spoke German and some Italian, and I was a huge help—I did dialects. The hotel restaurant had closed, so we couldn't even sign for a meal (except espressos, thank goodness). We were really awake, very hungry, and out of luck. Still, it was Italy, and most people would have been on top of the world. But I really missed my son. This was the first time I was ever away from my son Michael for very long—and this was Easter Sunday!

So what does one do in Milan on Easter? Go to church! We walked toward the cathedral, grateful for where we were (and trying to ignore our growling tummies). We turned a corner, and there it was: Il Domo cathedral. Our hearts stopped. It was so beautiful—and huge! As we entered, I wasn't ready for the spectacular sight—thousands of little, white flickering candles everywhere I turned. People knelt in prayer, and the choir sounded like angels! We all three burst into tears.

I will never forget the atmosphere in Il Domo that Easter Sunday. It inspired my home—and I'm always teased about how long it actually takes to light my candles before guests arrive.

In the spotlight

What is your favorite time of day? Your favorite time of year? Is it the mild haze of an early October morning? The bright midday sun of a clear May day? The warm glow of an August sunset? Or the deep black sky of a crisp December night? What is it about the light of this time of day or year that moves you?

Choose a specific type of light (a flickering candle, a lighthouse spotlight, buzzing fluorescent—anything) that describes your personality. How do you relate to this type of light? Are you happy with the "light you are," or would you rather make a change? What could you do to change your mood (lighting)?

Which type of light makes you feel energized, relaxed, exhausted, or romantic? Create a "light journal" to note how different types of light affect you.

Scent is one of the strongest senses tied to memory. What scent consistently evokes a specific memory for you?

When you're sweating bullets in the middle of a heat wave, what do you do? You lower the thermostat! Well I say music can be used as a thermostat too—an atmosphere thermostat! Sense perceptions—color, light, texture, scent—affect mood and alter our atmosphere. So does sound! When the party is dying and it needs a pick-me-up, what do you do? Pump up the volume and dance! After a day of meetings and traffic nightmares, we mellow out with a little jazz, or country, or Mozart. And doesn't R&B seem made for romance? Whether energizing, soothing, or seductive, music transforms us all. So turn on some tunes, and turn up the heat.

MUSIC
the atmosphere thermostat

MUSIC
the atmosphere thermostat

Music is *the* most incredible, amazing atmosphere thermostat. I can walk into any space and change the entire vibe simply by turning on music. So many people work to achieve a beautiful home but then don't truly experience it! They spend a fortune to make their home terrific but never install a decent entertainment system. Music is essential to our homes and lifestyles! It can ripple through a room with incredible power.

Think of music as your home's best friend. By turning a dial or pushing a button, you can fill the air to fit the mood, easily creating the atmosphere you desire in any space you want. In many ways, music is the most versatile lifestyle accessory. So decorate your room with sound. Whether you seek a sleek, metropolitan vibe, a relaxed laid-back atmosphere, or a mini tropical vacation by the pool, you can conjure the mood you want simply by selecting sounds that accessorize.

Music expresses that which cannot be said and on which it is impossible to be silent. —VICTOR HUGO

Music sets the atmosphere for any evening or occasion. Consider sporting events; music has become a major part of the experience. Vibrant, exciting, and intense, it sets the tone to get the crowd going and to rev up the team. What would a scary movie be like without the music that moves you to the edge of your seat? You'll find a song for every possible emotion. How cool is that?

In fact, listening to music gets us through different emotional states—times that we just need to let go and feel. A haunting melody or a certain lyric sometimes

breaks the dam, and all our emotions come pouring through. Music can be cathartic and cleansing, but it can also be just plain fun! It reflects and even alters who we are.

Are you a morning person? For some of us, music provides just that extra spunk we need to start the day—caffeine for the soul! Set the alarm clock to a station or song that gets you going, and see what a difference it makes. Of course, rock riffs in the morning aren't for everyone. Your rise 'n' shine tunes may be just the opening moments of the relaxation you need before you start the day. Try making your wake-up call an instrumental mix or classical compilation.

Music washes away from the soul the dust of everyday life. —RED AUERBACH

Now music is playing a role in your home—and you haven't even gotten out of bed yet! But music can carry us through the day. Mix up some musical compilations or buy some collections that can serve as the soundtrack for your life. Your soundtrack can keep you going—from soothing your jangly nerves to pumping you up for a night on the town! Let music be your driver when you're stuck in bumper-to-bumper traffic. Instead of getting caught up in road rage, find your groove and coast down the highway to the beat that fits your life!

Think "sound design"—decorate with sound and make your home express who you are. Just turn on the music!

My girlfriend Nancy Lacy and I used to shop at this little clothing store in Scottsdale, Arizona. Its name—Uh Oh—was perfect because we'd get into so much trouble! From the minute we walked in, we felt happy and lighthearted; we'd laugh and dance and spend hours hanging out! I realized that the music playing in the shop had a huge part in making us feel so comfortable and free! They had these fabulous compilation CDs that were all Motown's greatest hits—singers like Smokey Robinson, Aretha Franklin, Sam Cooke. How smart to play music that seems almost universally fun, fabulous, and upbeat!

Another place Nancy and I frequented was Santa Fe, New Mexico. One summer, we attended the "Buckeroo Ball," a charity event. Everyone wears anything, but cowboy boots and a concho belt are downright required. That year was really special because Nancy's favorite country star, Willie Nelson, was performing! I knew she was excited, but I had no idea just how much she had been looking forward to this. When the concert started, Nancy moved a bit closer and left me sitting at the table. Song after song went by, so I started pushing through the crowds to find her. I finally got up on the side of the stage to see into the crowd, and there was Nancy, front and center, singing and dancing her heart out. I'll never forget how free and full of joy she was!

Whenever we're together, we get a kick out of listening to some of our old favorites as we venture the highway, but none brings back such a carefree memory as Willie does!

TESTING, TESTING 1-2-3

Try this experiment for thirty days—one month! Pick out several CDs (or spend some time legally downloading some tunes)—music that makes you relax, that makes you feel romantic, that makes you want to dance or work on home projects, or conquer the day! Have music on hand for every possible situation that you have in your life. Start using music in a therapeutic way. Turn off your TV and *enjoy* your cup of coffee in the morning in front of your fireplace or on your porch with music that soothes your soul. Don't say you don't have time! Start by getting ready to go out for the evening by listening to your favorite song; be careful you don't become so lost in the music that you skip dinner completely! Or listen to a song that wakes you up and sets the tone to dance all night, or something that makes you feel like you can conquer the world as you travel to the office to clinch the big deal.

If you try this experiment, you'll see how much music improves your life! It will not only get you moving mentally, but physically too. I love the way Ellen DeGeneres starts every show with music and dancing. Even if it's just a head rockin' or a foot tappin', you will start to move to the beat.

UNCOMPLICATED COMPILATIONS

Looking for the perfect mix for your next get-together? Need some mood music to get you going in the morning?

I've done the legwork for you! Go to **www.mollandersonhome.com** to choose from a variety of party and lifestyle compilations. Whether it's a funky fiesta or a bridal brunch, music to romance your home or bring life to your bachelor pad, I've collected some of my favorites and put them together in one easy place.

With a click of a mouse, you'll see just how easy it is to control your atmosphere thermostat with your very own Moll Anderson Home Lifestyle CD!

—*Moll*

MUSICAL NOTES

If a full-throttle entertainment system isn't for you, then look to cable; often now you can have music in your home with the touch of your remote!

Several home stores have great compilation CDs, as do your favorite music stores. It's a quick way to have excellent party music if you don't have the time to mix your own CDs.

Movie soundtracks can provide a wonderful range of easy listening fare. Two of my favorites are *Living Out Loud* and *What Women Want*.

After silence, that which comes nearest to expressing the inexpressible is music.

—ALDOUS HUXLEY

Tune into you

If you could pick a theme song, what would it be? (If you can't pick just one song, make it a soundtrack to live by!)

_____

_____

_____

_____

_____

_____

_____

_____

_____

_____

Assign a song to each room in your home. What mood does that song set for you? Think about the atmosphere you want to create in each individual room, and give it a tune.

_____

_____

_____

_____

_____

_____

_____

_____

_____

_____

Think about your favorite genre of music. What images, colors, and experiences come to mind when you think of that type of music? Create a visual description of the musical genre, and consider this as a possible starting point for a room's inspiration.

Name one song to go with each of the following categories: Motivate, Relax, Focus, Romance, and Reflect.
Create more categories for yourself, and give them each a song as well!

You don't have to be a horticulturist to appreciate the beauty of blooms. From casual nosegays to exotic centerpieces, flowers have a powerful effect on your quality of life. They evoke sensory responses through both sight and smell, and have the potential to brighten the blandest of spaces—virtually instantly. These extraordinarily versatile accessories come in a variety of colors, sizes, and scents, perfect for a wide range of lifestyles. So stop and smell the roses— and then cut them for an arrangement!

say it with FLOWERS

say it with
FLOWERS

The designer's best friend, flowers immediately add a splash of color to any room and come in a wide array of varieties. From fresh-cut roses to earthy limbs such as pussy willow, from trailing ivy to the exotic blooms of orchids, there's a plant for any personality and occasion.

For a casual breakfast nook, and that fresh-from-the-market feel, try something simple like daisies or tulips. They'll add not only a bit of color to the table, but also an aroma that only fresh flowers can bring to a space.

In all things of nature there is something of the marvelous. —ARISTOTLE

For a dramatic entryway table, try arranging limbs from a flowering cherry tree or add a bit of exotic flare with dried ornamental grasses or large palm leaves (the freeze-dried ones will last forever). You can even add fruits and other organic elements.

Just as important as the flowers themselves is the way that the flowers are displayed. One neat trick is to use everyday household containers to present flowers. Sometimes smaller containers and simpler arrangements can make the biggest statement. Sterling silver sugar bowls, teacups, and even candle votives can make dashing displays for a couple of Gerber daisies in a not-so-dazzling powder room.

But what if you're planning a dinner party and want a floral display that's attractive yet not distracting? Begin with one simple question: How will my guests be seated?

FLOWERS
say it with

There's nothing worse than trying to peer through a labyrinth of lilies to talk with your dinner guests. Put away your traditional, tall vases and dig up shorter, wider containers to arrange your display. You don't have to limit yourself to conventional clear glass. Experiment with colored glass, porcelain, or metal containers. You can use anything—just be sure that you use a plastic liner if the item is not waterproof, or set the flowers into a glass container and then lower that into the chosen piece. Finish off the look by covering any open spaces with dried moss.

When it comes to choosing flowers, plan like you'd plan your menu. Think seasonal: berries, branches, and evergreens for a winter dinner; big blooms and bright colors for a summer brunch. Whatever the season, collect your flowers at least a day or two before your event to make sure they're open and as fresh as can be on the big day.

Finally, if you're having a dinner party, ask yourself what you want your guests to notice more, the aroma of the food or the powerful perfume of your floral display. Look for flowers and garnishes that have subtle scent or no scent at all. That way you don't overpower your food or your friends.

Another design trick for the decorator with a lot of style and just a little time is to use a year-round silk arrangement. Trust me! These aren't your grandmother's silk flowers. Today's silk arrangements offer a sophisticated alternative to fresh greenery. You can add your own "live" elements, and switch them out to suit your mood. For a summer brunch, insert some fresh lemons and bright blooms from the grocery store. For a dinner party in the fall, work in some curly willow, Leonardo roses, and pomegranates! You'll save lots of time (and money). Flowers freshen up every room. So get busy piling those posies in places you never thought about!

Moll

Jennifer Willey and I have been friends for years; we are very much alike and that puts us in situations that force us to follow through in big ways. Like volunteering! Jenn and I agreed to host a fundraiser for abused children (one of our most important interests). We knew we could do it, even without a cent in our budget.

It was early fall, and the night before the event. We had it all figured out—except what to do with the yard. Everything that had bloomed during spring and summer was not only dead, but really bare. We started by stringing every mini white-light set we could find and unearthing every candelabra I had ever found. We placed them everywhere. It really looked great—as long as it was dark. But people would be coming as early as 5:30; it was going to be light for a while.

Finally, exhausted, we reluctantly called it a night. At dawn, I woke up with the solution! I flew down to the basement to bring up containers full of gorgeous silk blooms left from another event. I filled pots, placed them under the trees, lined the walkway, put them around the Koi pond, in all the urns, and even in the flowerbed. All of a sudden, everything was coming up roses!

The fundraiser was a great success, and I can't tell you how many people commented on my amazing flowers and yard. Was it a miracle? Maybe, but I think it was also the magic of flowers.

I love the huge orchid arrangements in hotels and fashion magazines. But those arrangements can cost hundreds of dollars. Here's a quick and easy trick that will give you a luxurious orchid arrangement right in your own home.

1 Choose a large container. It can be anything from a leather box to a ceramic urn. The idea is to be able to plant several orchids into it comfortably. So choose the number of orchids you want, and then determine the size of the container.

2 Pick up your potted orchids at your local nursery or home-improvement center. I always like to use odd numbers—try three or five.

3 Water the orchids and allow them to drain.

4 Keep the orchids in their separate little pots, but arrange them in the large container.

5 Place wadded up newspaper all around and in between the orchids to fill space and to hold the plants in place.

6 Place a generous amount of moss all over the top of the container so that all you see are the stems of the orchids coming up out of the container. The idea is for it to look as though you have one large orchid plant.

Now you can enjoy the beauty of your sophisticated orchids for weeks to come! (This also works well with other potted plants. Put poinsettias in one large basket during the holiday season, or use mums in the fall.)

SHOPPING LIST

Large container

Orchids (at least three)

Several bags of green moss (available at art supply and home-improvement centers)

Newspaper

Plastic plant liner from the nursery (to fit your container)

FLOWER POWER

Did you know that scientists have actually proven that flowers have a positive effect on people? Sure, we all know that we feel better when we receive flowers or have them around the house, but a Rutgers University study has proven it. Not only do people reap positive benefits such as heightened satisfaction and decreased anxiety when they receive flowers as a gift, but when flowers are displayed in the home, people perceive their presence as symbolic of sharing, and in turn consider the space to be more welcoming. So put those flowers in prominent spots and share the positive effects of flowers with your family and guests!

FLOWER FACTS

Well Packaged

Roses have what is termed packing petals—pull off the outside petals of your roses so they can bloom to their fullest.

Cut Clue

Always cut flower stems on the diagonal and immerse them immediately in water (or else the cut will close up!). When changing the water in your arrangement, always recut the stems.

Stem Sauna

If your party occurs before your flowers are fantastic, immerse the cut ends of stems in warm water so the blooms will open up faster!

Bloom Buzz

Tulips love vodka! Add a capful of vodka (a capful of bleach works, too) to your tulip water. It will keep the water clean and your tulips looking fresh.

Gardens and flowers have a way of

The Language of Flowers

TRADITIONALLY, FLOWERS HAVE MEANINGS
SO YOU CAN LITERALLY SAY IT WITH FLOWERS

Red Rosebud: A Confession of Love

Red Rose: Love and Passion

Pink Rose: Beauty

White Rose: Silence

Orchid: Beauty

Violet: Faithfulness

Purple Lilac: First Emotions of Love

Ivy: Friendship and Marriage

Hibiscus: Delicate Beauty

Daisy: Innocence

White Lily: Purity

Forget-Me-Not: True Love

White Chrysanthemum: Truth

Daffodil: Unrequited Love

Yellow Lily: Flirty

Chrysanthemum: Cheerfulness

Delphinium: Lightness

Sunflower: False Riches

Striped Carnation: Refusal

Pansy: Remembrance

Azalea: Self-control

Iris: A Message

Camellia: Loveliness

Zinnia: Absent Friends

bringing people together, drawing them from their homes.

—CLARE ANSBERRY

QUICK CHANGE ARTISTS

Using a standard year-round arrangement is not only a fantastic way to include flowers in your home every day, but it's also an easy way to throw together a dramatic look literally in minutes. Since fresh flowers can be costly, adding just a few when needed to a silk arrangement means saving not only time but money, too!

Shopping List

Vases

(I love using large, clear glass vases so that I can showcase the space inside.)

Silk flowers

(Don't be afraid to twist and bend them; make them look natural!)

Branches

(Try curly willow and redbud.)

Seasonal switch-outs

(Fruit works great, as do river rocks and moss.)

Fresh flowers

(You don't need many to make a bold statement.)

Start by buying or creating your year-round basic arrangement. In a vase, arrange your natural-looking silk flowers (you'll be amazed at some of the options out there now), along with some branches to add interest and height. Consider placing some moss at the base of your vase to give a splash of excitement to the bottom of the arrangement (it will look more finished if you do).

To spice it up a bit when you're having company over—or if the mood just strikes you—add some seasonal fruit or other filler to the vase! Think lemons for spring, pomegranates for fall, cranberries for winter, or river rocks for summer! As the months, or your moods, change, so can your arrangement. Finally, add some fresh blooms, and *voila!* An arrangement that's not just beautiful but easy and inexpensive, too.

ANYTHING GOES

Contrary to popular belief, there are *no rules* when it comes to flower arranging. Throw out the idea that arrangements have to be done "a certain way." (You know what I mean, "...Start with the tallest flowers first....") Be creative; what do *you* want to display in your arrangement? Grab some flowering branches off your trees, stick them in a rustic wood vase, and create an organic look! Toss some lemons, limes, green apples, or pomegranates into a clear glass bowl, and enjoy a sweet splash of color! Or fill a tall glass cylinder with some river rocks and water, and float a few orchid blooms for a simple yet dramatic centerpiece. If you're a sports fan, throw some baseballs into a bowl and *that* can be your arrangement! The key is to have fun while bringing some of the outside in. A flower arrangement doesn't have to have flowers—it just has to inspire you.

The secret garden

What is your favorite type of foliage? Do you love fresh-cut garden flowers or vibrant tropicals?
Large lush blooms or bare branches?

Pick the flower that best fits your personality. What is it about that particular flower that stands out to you?
Is it the color, the scent, the place it grows, or its meaning?

Year-round silk plants are a great way to keep your flower arrangements easy! Just by adding various seasonal elements, or something you have around the house, you can quickly transform the look of your arrangement—and your room. Even if you don't have a year-round silk arrangement, imagine that you do. Now mentally hunt through your house for items that you could use to spruce up your arrangement. What can you use? Remember, anything goes!

Fresh flowers need not be limited to a traditional vase. Set your imagination on a scavenger hunt through your home. What might be used to hold flowers, branches, or fruits? Think beyond that basic arrangement—be bold—you might just uncover your next spectacular idea!

One of the most telling elements in a home, fabric adds texture and so much personality. From natural linens and casual cottons to luxurious leathers and lush velvets, fabric provides the ultimate final touch. And that bit of pizzazz really spices up the style in your space. One of the few design elements geared to the sense of touch, fabric welcomes you with comfort. So take a clue from your closet and cover your couch with that decadent cashmere. Play dress-up with your decorating, and find a fabric that fits your mood.

FABRIC *by the bolt*

FABRIC *by the bolt*

Fashion magazines bulge with pages of luxurious clothing. Leathers, suedes, velvets, mohair, and cashmere—rich, wonderful textures. And every one of the fabrics that designers choose for their haute couture lines can translate from the runway directly to a sofa, chair, or drapes in your home.

Designers know this, too. Giorgio Armani, Ralph Lauren, Donna Karan, and Tom Ford are already blurring the line between fashion and furniture. They've all expanded their fashion collections to the home. And why not? The clothing they design is timeless and made of fabrics that last a lifetime. Perfect for the home!

Were we to apply the same fashion rules to our homes that we do to our wardrobes, we'd make smarter choices. For instance, our "investment" furniture should be a design that will stand the test of time. A sofa with spectacular lines can be reupholstered decade after decade—updated by simply changing the fabric.

The fabrics, whether it be hand-painted prints at the end, or whether it be new knits and stretch fabrics... sort of make the whole world. —RALPH LAUREN

Whether buying for the first time or reupholstering, select fabric that satisfies your sense of touch. Then choose your colors for your sofa or chairs with a classic palette in mind. My classic black wool suit stands the test of time, and I'm able to change it in an instant by adding a new, colorful blouse or beautiful scarf. Toss new pillows or a throw on the sofa and chairs to spice up an elegant,

Moll Anderson client

classic design. If you go with bold prints or wacky colors for the furniture upholstery, you're likely to tire of them easily. But do go with the color that draws you.

Don't get me wrong; sometimes you just *have* to cut loose and go trendy! If you can afford the red crocodile-print side chair, then go for it. I must admit I've got quite a few trendy items in my closet alongside the diehard classics—mostly because I got a fantastic deal on them somewhere. And you'll probably find an unusual piece of furniture or two around my house, as well. I love to bargain shop, whether it's a flea market or an antique store, a great sale or a discount outlet, it's all about the hunt! But I definitely started with the basics, and these basics are still with me years later as my home continues to evolve.

Whether you're looking for fabric to make window treatments, pillows, or throws or to upholster your furniture, if you make good, solid choices, classic pieces can follow you from your first apartment to a condo to your dream home. In your home, as well as your wardrobe, a few essential classics let you create a look that's casual, trendy, romantic, or sophisticated, simply by adding the right accessories.

Always think about your lifestyle when choosing fabrics to live on. If you have

When I don't have any ideas, I pick up fabric and start working with it and something happens.

—GEOFFREY BEENE

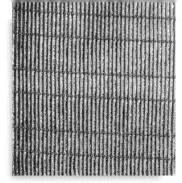

small children, think at least twice before purchasing white linen. Do you really want to be watching over the furniture instead of your children? With hundreds of fabrics and every color and texture to choose from, you can pick the ones that are family friendly and that accomplish just the effect you want. So take some time and think about what you need when investing in furniture and fabrics.

Don't ignore the bed! After all, that's where we spend nearly a third of our lives. And nothing beats the luxury of good linens when you crawl into your bed. So if you haven't taken high thread counts seriously yet, it's way past time. I call it the CPN factor—cost per night—when I'm talking about sleep. If you split the cost over years, then it becomes worth it. I love the Italian linens by Frette; they are the luxury item I so long aspired to have!

So find your ultimate fabrics and give them the real test: Would you want to wear a piece of clothing out of it? If you do, there's a pretty good chance that they are perfect for your home. Fabrics don't have to be expensive—you just have to want to touch them!

Moll

Years ago, I bought an amazing Armani suit. My "investment" was wise. It's a classic, untrendy staple in my wardrobe, and one I've never regretted buying. (I call this CPW—cost per wear!) I always travel with it, and besides wearing it traditionally, I can use the jacket with jeans and a t-shirt or skirt, and the slacks with a sweater. I can funk it up or class it out! It's made of a gorgeous black wool—an important basic for my wardrobe.

I thought, why should it be any different in my home? So I put it to the test; I made several sets of drapes for four rooms—three homes ago—and they have traveled with me from Arizona to Tennessee. The trick is that I made them in classic fabrics that I loved. One set is chocolate mohair, another a rich plum velvet, a third set is cognac wool, and the last is a woven earthy chenille.

I made all the drapery panels double widths of fabric and two feet longer than I needed. Since then I have split a couple of panels to cover an extra window or two; I just tuck them under when they're a bit too long and hang them as high as possible, which makes my ceiling feel higher. Or, somtimes I've just gone for the dramatic puddle effect.

So just like a favorite suit that needs only a bit of updating or alterations, my drapes continue to keep hanging around.

WEAR THE ROOM

If you're redecorating, one incredible piece is all it takes. You might choose a magnificent rug, a unique sculpture, or a gorgeous armoire. That one piece can make an entire room. It might even be the inspiration for decorating the rest of the room. If you're having custom drapes, pillows, upholstery, or slipcovers made, then make sure you're knocked out by the fabric. My rule is that I have to be so blown away by the feel of the fabric that I would want to wear a piece of clothing made out of it! So take a walk through your closet and see what clothing you have that could translate to a room in your home. What attracts you may be the color, texture, or the print. Whatever it is, that just might be the starting point for your new room.

MODEL HOME

Photograph or sketch a room in your home that you would like to redesign. Blow up the image using a copy machine so that it's large enough for you to work with. Using a fashion magazine, cut out "swatches" of fabric from clothing that catches your eye and use it to "reupholster" your room! Make the curtains the sheer flowy skirt on one page and the couch the leather jacket on another. Go crazy and experiment—it's only paper! If your "fabric swatch" is too small for the space you need, manufacture more by making a color copy or filling it in with colored pencils and markers. Use your model room page to guide you regarding fabric and color choices when you really go shopping.

Part of the wonderful thing about what we do in fashion is that it really can apply to so many forms of one's lifestyle, and it is such a logical extension to be designing for the home. —CALVIN KLEIN

IN THE DOGHOUSE

When I design a home, it has to be livable for everyone—including pets. Your home is meant to be where you can relax and put your feet up. If you spend all of your time scolding pets (or kids!) for touching this piece of furniture or going into that room, then you're definitely not truly *living* in or enjoying your space.

Of course there should be boundaries—it's just that when you're in a house that you constantly have to worry about, you're no fun to be around. Nobody in your home will ever truly experience the meaning of "sanctuary" if you're upset about the latest spill, muddy print, or furball. And I don't mean putting plastic on your sofas and chairs! Choose pet-friendly fabrics. Use textures and tones that won't show sticky fingers, shedding hair, or wet paws.

A few simple solutions will help make your home more child- and pet-friendly and your pet more home-friendly. You *can* have a drop-dead gorgeous home that's low maintenance if you plan well.

The Master of Disguise

Try mohair! The first movie theaters chose mohair to cover the seats because of its durability. In fact, it's not a sacrifice in a way because it's both luxurious and cleanable. It repels dust and dirt, plus comes in gorgeous colors. Darker is better at camouflage-duty, but consider the color of your pet. If you have a golden retriever, don't go with slate or espresso!

Another shed-solution is to keep a faux-fur throw on the corner of a couch. That way your pet has its own place to perch. After all, Spot needs a spot too!

Flooring is another major aspect of a pet-friendly home. It's obvious that bright white carpeting is probably not the most practical choice for pet-owners (or anyone for that matter). If you just have to have something soft under your feet, go with area rugs that have texture or pattern. Otherwise, keep your floors simple and clean-up friendly. Hardwoods, laminates, and vinyl can help keep your home looking fresh.

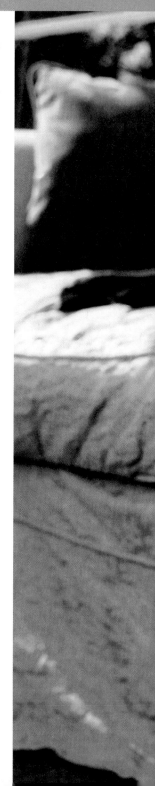

As a designer, one of my favorite decorating tools is pillows. They are the quickest way to spice up any space in a snap. When you're considering pillows, think color, pattern, and texture. Toss out those matching pillows that come standard with your neutral couch. Make a statement with bright, contrasting colored pillows in silks or cottons. A great way to pull a room together is by using a pillow with a pattern that ties together all the tones of the room. Pillows can also be a great way to add seasonal touches to a room. For instance, rich chocolate browns or pumpkin for fall, crisp white linen for spring, or Mediterranean blues for summer.

But pillows can be quite costly, especially if they are custom designed. So make your own! Here's a cool trick that won't break the bank; it will just look that good.

1 Lay the fabric out, folded in half.

2 Cut a perfect square.

3 Turn the fabric square finished-side down on a flat surface, and place the foam insert in the center.

4 Gather the fabric up and around the insert until you surround the insert.

5 Use a heavy rubber band to gather the fabric—like putting hair in a ponytail.

6 Adjust the pleating around the pillow, and then trim the top.

7 Wrap some decorative cord around the rubber band, and tie it into a bow.

Different fabrics make different statements about your room. Toile gives a classic, formal feel. Suede sends a more luxurious message. And denim denotes a casual, family look.

In minutes, you can make a simple accent pillow that adds style and fun to your furniture.

SHOPPING LIST

Fabric
(the amount of fabric depends upon the size of your foam insert; measure enough to cover the insert completely, plus more for the pleating when the fabric is pulled up and over it)

Round foam insert

Ties, tassels, or cords

Scissors

Heavy rubber bands

Measuring tape

CURTAIN CALL

A shower curtain can almost furnish a bathroom, so put a little extra thought into it. Why settle for a store-bought shower curtain when there are so many gorgeous drapes in wonderful fabrics to choose from? The basic supplies for this project are easily found in the bath department of any discount or bed & bath store.

You're actually hanging two curtains (the inner plastic liner and the outer curtain), so the first step is to decide how long you want your gorgeous outer curtain to be. I like to hang the outer curtain from ceiling to floor to add height and drama to the room. Make your decision and measure accordingly before you purchase the drapes you'll use as your outer curtain. Then, just hang them up for instant glam!

CHOOSE FABRICS LIKE THE PROS

Picking out fabric is often such a daunting task because people get bogged down in "what it is." Here's my insider tip about how to pick fabric like the pros: Touch it! No need to read the fine print on the back of the fabric tag; if it feels good, and you like the way it looks, buy it.

SHOPPING LIST

Clear plastic shower curtain liner
One standard adjustable curtain rod
(for the clear plastic liner)
Second curtain rod (for the drapes)
You can use a second adjustable rod to hang the drapes, but any kind of curtain rod will work. Consider wrought iron or steel, or maybe a wooden rod; you can refinish it just like you would for drapes in any other room.
Shower curtain rings
(any color or style you prefer)
Drapes
Don't get ready-made shower curtains; select ready-made drapes instead. Choose a beautiful fabric that strikes your fancy—something you'd never expect to see in a bathroom. Since the clear plastic liner will keep the fabric from getting wet, you can use drapes in just about any fabric you'd like—from velvet to silk.

Yard by yard

If you could pull any item from your closet and cover your couch in it, what would it be? Your favorite holey t-shirt? Your floor-length faux-fur jacket? What is it about this item that you love?

List your favorite clothing designers or clothing stores. What is it about brands that you love? The classic tailoring, the luxurious materials, the wild colors? What keeps you coming back to these designers or stores?

Go into a fabric store and get swatches of three favorite fabrics. Don't think about where they will go in a room, or what they will be used for. Just pick out fabrics that you like! Store them inside this book and revisit them every once in a while. What draws you the most? Do you still love them after you've had them a while?

Pick two pairs of shoes: one from your closet that represents your current lifestyle and the other from a magazine that represents a lifestyle you desire. Describe these two pairs of shoes on three levels: function, quality, and style. How do they differ? What do you like about the pair that you currently own? What do you like about the "dream pair?"

Just because you lease doesn't make where you live less of a home. If you feel as though your dwelling isn't really your space, then you will always feel disconnected. Even when you don't *literally* *own* the space, you can still *emotionally* *own* it. Your home should ground you, be your safe haven, that place you can't wait to get to, the spot where you want to entertain friends. So whether you live in an apartment, condo, house, duplex, or even a dorm room, keep in mind that "home is truly where the heart is"— not where the mortgage is.

A new LEASE *on life*

T he greatest investment you can make in your life is in *you*. Even if you think that the space you live in isn't worth the investment—*you are*. Improve your living space to the best of your abilities because it affects you around the clock. This truly is a small investment with a *huge* return in lifestyle.

Owning a home of your own is the "American Dream." As soon as you're out on your own, you start saving until the day you can own, but until then, a rental it is. Some of us have already owned property, but circumstances find us renting once again. Whatever your situation might be, toss out the old thinking that tells you not to spend money on property you don't own. Think about your life right now; that's what really matters! (I call it CPL—cost per living. It's about the balance between what something costs vs. what you get out of it.)

Some paint, dimmer switches, elbow grease, and a little know-how are all it takes! Wherever you live (and within the confines of the lease agreement!), make it your home. Do whatever is comfortable for you, but do something! Achieve an environment that you can feel good about.

When I was living in a rental house, I did everything I could to make it feel like home. I stripped wallpaper, faux-finished the walls, and painted every square inch of that house. I redid the woodwork, put new hardware on the cabinets, and, yes, added dimmer switches everywhere possible! I poured my heart into making the place where I lived *my* home.

Create a warm, inviting environment that reflects who you are, or who you want to be. Take ownership of the space emotionally, and do the best with what you have.

If your landlord allows it, painting a wall or two is one of the easiest ways to make your mark on a space. Whether it's a bold color or a soothing hue,

Come live in my heart and pay no rent.

—SAMUEL LOVER

seeing a color that you love—a color that you chose—will help you to start to *live* in that space (not just rent it).

If your landlord won't budge on a new coat of paint (see my tips on negotiating), invest in stunning drapes instead! If you can't find the color you had your heart set on in a pair already made, try custom dying drapes with a mix of several commercial dyes (such as RIT) that you can get at the grocery store. Select drapes in machine-washable fabrics like cotton. Keep in mind that store-bought drapes are often a tad on the short side and may not offer the dramatic look you're going for. To make up for the lapse in length, consider sewing a complementary band of fabric at the base of the purchased drapes that you dyed. Or skip the dying altogether and pick a fabric that adds a color kick on its own. Since you're using only a yard or two, rather than the whole length of the window, you can really splurge and pick a fabric that makes a "statement" for just a little more. (Think faux leather, velvet, or silk!)

The floor is another area where rentals tend to be a bit bland and worn. If you're stuck with a not-so-great rug or a floor that looks older than you are, walk on the wild side! Area rugs are the perfect solution because they not only camouflage, but also put some punch into a space. They cover bare floors as well as dirty old carpets. So don't ignore the floor; it's the foundation of every room!

These quick and cost-effective changes will help you relax into and really *live* in your space. After all, this is your home, and your home reflects your soul. So create the life you want to live, wherever you are—and give yourself a new lease on life!

Moll

I love traveling back to Scottsdale, Arizona. What makes it so special are my friends and family. My mother is not living in the house I grew up in, but it's my "family home" now because my mom lives there. It's so comforting to sit in the chair my dad used to read in, or glance at the photos of my brother Bill and me before our braces—and long before we knew how lucky we were to have each other! What makes it home is what my mother taught us without even realizing it. You see, we teach our children by example.

My mother made every place we rented a fabulous home, even when it was a tiny apartment. It was always warm and cozy, clean and beautifully put together—stylish despite the budget. We finally did move into a gorgeous house (that we owned!) in Scottsdale the summer I turned thirteen. I had my own room, and we had a few more thousand square feet, but until Mom wove her magic, it was just bigger. Mom made it home.

I was a divorced single mom for years. Times were tough, and I learned to create a home on practically nothing. If you're a single dad or mom and living in a small apartment, rest assured your child doesn't care that you can't afford more right now. They, and you, need to feel secure there. Your home, be it ever so humble, can and should be a cozy little paradise.

Your children won't remember if you rented unless you tell them. They'll simply remember a place they called home.

TRADE SECRETS

CHEAP TRICKS

Dated or cheap paneling may be the one thing that's hard to avoid in rentals. If the landlord's not in love with that old look, consider textured paint finishes. Ralph Lauren's "Suede" finish really looks great. Venetian plaster is also an incredible look and easy to apply. A few generous coats will fill and cover those lines that show up under paint.

When making custom drapes, always sew double panels and extra lengths for heavy puddling. When you move, you can split the panels and make two sets of drapes from one if needed. The length won't be an issue. It's a safe investment!

One way to update in a flash is to install new hardware for the kitchen cabinets. Appliance paint is also fabulous. It covers nicks and rust stains on old stoves, ovens, and dishwashers to create a clean, fresh look.

If your kitchen floor happens to be a colorful wild pattern from who knows what era (and you can't replace it), don't fight it! Work with it. Choose the best color from the floor and paint your walls to take the emphasis off that wacky pattern. You can always pick up inexpensive rugs to cover the majority of the flooring.

Update your fireplace immediately by replacing those old brass-and-glass built-in covers. To dress up the room with a touch of sophistication, choose a fireplace screen of wrought iron or perforated tin instead, or install a mirror in the space.

Old homes often don't have great closet space, but don't think small. Turn an extra room into a walk-in closet simply by adding rolling racks and shelving.

Many a man who pays rent all his life owns his own home; and many a family has successfully saved for a home only to find itself at last with nothing but a house.
—BRUCE BARTON

NEGOTIATION:
THE PATH OF LEASE RESISTANCE

It's important to have a rapport with the landlord. Life is short, and you don't want to spend it at odds with your landlord. You don't have to be good friends, but you do need to communicate.

Start by discussing what they are planning to do before you move in. Most of the time, they plan to clean the carpets and hit the walls with a fresh coat of paint. But I was often surprised how many didn't plan doing a single thing. This kind of landlord works only if they are open to changes you want to make that will improve the property. (Keep it simple, though; don't freak out potential landlords with grandiose ideas.)

If you can see the space before it's painted, you can sometimes choose the colors. Offer to paint if they buy the paint and you select the colors. They save paying a painter, which is the more expensive part of the deal. If they have just painted everything white and it doesn't work for you, ask for permission to repaint, at no cost to them. Make sure you add to the lease you have

their consent. If they are afraid that your color choices might get out of hand, agree in writing that you will repaint any room that they designate. Most rentals, especially older properties, show so much better with rich color on the walls.

See if you can barter property improvements for a rent reduction. The more you improve it, the more rent your landlord will be able to get for the property's next lease. If you are a professional in the home-improvement area, you have the best shot at getting your rent reduced by trading improvements.

The bottom line is to state your case why you will be a great tenant, so use what you can: references from other landlords, pictures from improvements you've done in the past, your ideas for the space. Be sure to get any agreed-upon improvements (either by you or the landlord) in writing.

Just because you lease

List those things that you would like to change about your space—
everything! Divide the list into things that you can do on your own, and
things that you need your landlord's permission to do.

Do you feel like your leased space is home? List the things you've done to make yours feel like home.
Or write about what is holding you back. What can you do to take emotional ownership of the space?

What are your favorite things about your rental? What are the elements that are right about it? List them!
Think about why you picked that particular space over the others that you looked at. Was it the tall ceilings? The location?
The rent amount? Highlight what drew you to this space in the first place.

What is the biggest eyesore in your leased space? Using what you've learned in this chapter,
write about or sketch what you can do to camouflage that design dilemma.

Are some of you guys out there waiting until later to get married, but don't want to wait to create your own special home? Or how about some of you dads? Are you suddenly single and starting over in a territory that's completely foreign to you and your kids? No matter what your situation is, whether you're on your own for the first time or moving into a new place with your kids after a divorce, you're officially a bachelor. And as we all know, every bachelor needs his pad. It doesn't matter whether it's an apartment, condo, or dorm room, or kids or no kids, this is your Bachelor Pad.

bachelor pad, bachelor DAD

bachelor pad, bachelor DAD

Unless you are completely blessed with the designer gene, you are probably feeling a little lost with what seems like an overwhelming amount of decisions as far as your space goes. Where do you begin? What paint choices do you make? How do you make that old sofa your parents gave you work? How are you going to entertain with Tonka toys and Barbies everywhere? How do you make a good decision about purchasing classic furniture so your cool new condo stays cool (and not boring)?

First, don't panic!

Design is about paying attention to all the little things that truly make a difference in your lifestyle, and *that's* what really transforms any space into a home.

You guys may not realize it, but you're already gifted with the ability to pay attention to details. Think about it: When you plan a Super Bowl party, I'm sure you don't forget the television, cable, inviting all your buds, and making sure that your beverages are all in order, along with setting up plenty of food! See, you guys have been natural party planners all along.

So keeping that in mind, you just need to apply similar thought to how you are going to approach your new digs. Details, details, details! I'm here to help you. We can make the most of whatever you've got! Whether we hide it, camouflage it, or embellish it—I've got loads of ideas.

Most important, remember that you can do anything that you set your mind to. If you want a home that you can really *live* in, then take a little time to figure

out what it is you need and want from your space. This really isn't all that difficult. It's about digging deep and searching for the things that you're attracted to and figuring out how to incorporate them into your home and life. We're talking about colors, textures, and vibes.

Guys are actually easier to figure out than the ladies. Men are always quick to tell me what their favorite color is, while the girls hem and haw and have several reasons for why they like a certain color for certain things. So think about why you like a certain color. Is that blue the same color of eyes of a girl you had a crush on in school? Or maybe that red that you're completely crazy about was the color of a Mustang that you dreamed about driving (but were only fourteen)? Perhaps that fishing trip to the lake with your family made a huge impact on you when you were surrounded by the lush green trees, tranquil lake, and rustic lodge, and now you're thinking about bringing the mountains home to your city life.

Whatever you're attracted to, I can guarantee there's a connection to something, someplace, or someone. So start paying attention and dig up those memories; you might even find a few new favorites you've simply forgotten about. You can start simple by first using paint to change the energy of one room and work from there. Before you know it, you'll be really living in your space!

Moll

I've never seen more stuff than when my good friend Judy Hogue and I helped our sons move into their first apartment in college. My son Mike and her son John had been friends since the fourth grade, and now they were going to college and living in one of our ultimate vacation destinations: San Diego!

Unfortunately, the high cost of living meant they got a lot less space for our money! The theme for their apartment was all the stuff they had—TVs, CDs, videos, stereos, sports gear, and computers.

So we ran to the nearest multi-purpose, get-everything store and got all the essentials: dishes, flatware, towels, sheets and bedding, microwave, laundry detergent, and all the clutter control containers we could fit into our cars. We had a blast, and at the same time, none of us were talking about what was really about to happen. Judy and I were going to leave our sons to live on their own in another state! Well, we organized them and gave thousands of directions on how to do this and how to do that. We made up their beds and set up their bathrooms. We did everything we could possibly do and dragged it out for as long as we could until it was time to leave. Our boys had grown up, and we were saying good-bye to them the way mothers do. It would never ever be the same again.

BACHELOR DAD

What can you do to make the most of your space when your kids have taken over? Create a room or bedroom for them that is specifically oriented for their enjoyment. Let them take part in helping to create this special room so that they will truly have a connection to you and your home—especially if you have joint custody. They need to feel as though they have a place in your heart *and* home.

If your funds are limited and you have only one bedroom, that makes it a bit tougher but not impossible. Consider a daybed or trundle bed in the living room that can easily be disguised when it's not your weekend for the kids. It's important for you to keep your own bedroom space during this transition. That way, if you enter into a new relationship, your children won't feel as though you have kicked them out of your room.

Make this experience of creating their own space fun by allowing them to pick their own bedding and keep pajamas, some clothes, a toothbrush, and all the other essentials there to make them feel at home. Be sure they have toys and special items, as well. Computers have become essential to doing homework. If you can swing it, consider a computer for them a priority. They need to be able to easily go back and forth between homes and not disrupt their schoolwork.

Clutter control is how you manage your life between being a dad and a bachelor with your own life. Think in terms of dual-purpose furniture with hidden compartments for toys and all the other stuff you want to keep out of the way. Ottomans with a lid will work, as will great leather boxes with lids that can double as an end table when stacked. A trunk can be used as a toy chest, as well as a coffee table. You get the idea.

You choose how to live your life and how your circumstances will dictate your lifestyle. You *can* be a dad and a bachelor, too!

BACHELOR

This is it, the first real space that you can call your own. Even if it's just a bed and shelves in a dorm room, it's yours! But maybe you're just *existing* (compared to *living*) in your condo or apartment. The truth is, you're making a mistake by not creating a place that you look forward to coming home to and truly living in. You might even think that it doesn't really matter—you're happy the way things are.

Do any of these life situations apply to you: you're starting over after the end of a relationship; you're waiting to have a significant other to work with you; you're "stuck" and can't move forward; you simply don't want to make a mistake.

So you do nothing. Whatever—it's time to start figuring out why you may not be truly *experiencing* your space.

I'll bet that the cable works and the TV is visible from your bed (or kitchen—or both). But I'll also bet that you haven't bought that couch you've been looking at every weekend at your favorite furniture store, or you haven't unpacked all your boxes. Who needs pots and pans—you eat out every night! And who really wants to wash them afterwards? Maybe all you need to do is finally hang those pictures that are still lying against the hallway wall. A good friend of mine, who was a great designer himself, once had—for more than a year—three different colors of paint brushed all over an entry wall where you entered his home. He couldn't decide which color was the best! He had things that were undone everywhere. The result was that he didn't love his space, and that created chaos, and that affected his life. If this is the case in your life, then you're simply occupying some square footage—and that's not the same as living in your home.

You need a *lifestyle makeover.*

Start simple, and take it one step at a time. Include my five must-haves and some of my tips to get your bachelor pad rocking!

PROJECT

Help Your TV Stand Out!

If you have a TV and no stand, get it off the floor! Build a simple, open TV stand or entertainment center with the help of your friendly hardware store. If you can handle a hammer, nails, and wood, you're off cheap and easy. Don't hesitate to ask for help or to try.

You can also use gray cement block for that Frank Lloyd Wright look. Just lay wood for shelves, painted in the same shade of gray. Place blocks the desired length apart and top with the shelf, then put two more blocks on top of the shelf directly over the other blocks.

Inexpensive metal shelving units of every size are easy to find. Use one in just about any room for a quick and basic entertainment center. If the color doesn't suit you, spray-paint the whole unit (be sure to use paint that's suitable for metal).

Check out the thrift stores for old bookcases of all sizes and used entertainment centers. Just paint them the color you like!

If you do have a little money to spend, an entertainment center is a great investment piece. Search for great deals on pieces imported from Mexico, in antique stores, and in the classifieds.

Transform Your Old Speaker!

Don't throw out that old broken speaker! It makes a great stand for a small TV or an end table. Just cover it. The quickest fix is contact paper—it comes in many colors, even faux wood grain. (If you're in doubt, use black.) You can also use a staple gun to cover a speaker with fabric. For a more modern approach, consider nailing on thin sheets of metal. Home-improvement stores can cut them to size (ask for appropriate nails and take the speaker with you).

Modernize That Beat-Up Armoire!

Do you have an old armoire with the doors off-kilter or falling apart? Take them off and use the armoire as an entertainment center or computer desk, even as a wonderful bookshelf. It's a terrific storage solution—and looks great! But drill a hole in the back of the armoire for the cords. There's nothing worse than seeing unsightly cords coming out from all sides, so hide them.

Make Those Built-Ins Work for You!

I once turned a bay window with a built-in window seat and bookcases into an entertainment center. The window seat became the platform for the TV and large speakers. You can still use what you have (even if you don't have a bay window!). The key is to create a wall that houses your equipment and looks cool. Paint the shelves (and any other built-ins) the color of the TV (slate gray or black oil-base paint, in most cases). This works best if you have a large-screen TV. If your space doesn't have a window seat, then just let the large screen stand on its own between the bookcases or you can build a simple wood box platform.

Arrange the equipment (stereo, amplifier, video, DVD, additional speakers) the way you desire. Use leftover shelves for CDs, videos, and DVDs. The better you line these up to size, the spiffier they look! Don't be afraid to add books and photos to break up the boxy rows.

If you have a small TV, build or place your equipment around it so the emphasis is off the TV and on the entertainment center itself. Cover any windows behind the TV. Black paper shades work beautifully. They are sold folded accordion style, and you cut each end to size with scissors. Black plastic clips adjust up and down, and there's a self-adhesive strip. It doesn't get any easier than that.

Closet Your Custom Entertainment Center!

Do you have a tiny bedroom closet too small to house your clothes? Then it's just the right size for a hideaway entertainment center. I did this myself. My interior closet space was triangular-shaped, so I cut a template from newspaper. Do that, or just measure. Then let your local home-improvement store cut the number of boards you need. Decide how many by considering how much equipment you need to stack. Paint the inside of the closet and shelves black.

In my little triangular closet, I used my sub-woofer for the base and placed one of the boards on top of it. Then I placed my TV on top of that board. I placed another board on top of my TV, then stacked my video and amplifier on top of that one. I put the third board on top of a half shelf that was already permanently fastened to the closet. That's where I stored my CDs and videos.

For a more finished look, you can mount brackets on the inside of the closet so that the shelves are suspended. It's really not much more effort and looks much cleaner.

Stack and Store Your Stuff!

An old metal school locker is a neat way to store CDs and videos—or just about anything else—and they don't take up a lot of space. Paint is key here. Use a spray paint designed for metal. And don't play it safe! Choose firehouse red or cobalt blue. If you have a set of attached lockers, all the better. It just makes for more storage.

Do you have a ton of books and magazines but no way to shelve them right now? Stack them! Put them under coffee tables, sofa tables, and benches. The key is to make the piles neat and group them by size, facing the same direction—like you meant to do it.

Think "creative container" when you decide what to do with all those disks and videos. Consider straw or hand-woven rattan boxes. You'll find boxes in leather and colored heavy cardboard. Stacked on top of each other, they add an interesting design element to the room. There are file-sized boxes, as well. They look chic on a shelf and hide any clutter.

Garage sales and flea markets are goldmines for the small end tables and boxes that can house your tapes and disks. Make sure you throw one of each—DVD, CD, video—in the car so you can check the fit.

Dressers provide a cool way to hide these items. It's easy to make dividers for the drawers. Decide how you want to position the tapes and CDs inside the drawer; then have pieces of wood cut to the right size to divide them. They're simple and quick to install.

Show Off Those LPs!

If you have a record collection, treat those LPs to their own long, low record case. The size can differ according to the size of the collection you have and, of course, how much space is available. Just measure the space where you plan to put the case. Make it as deep as the albums and at least 2 inches higher.

Head out to your favorite home-improvement center with the following: an album, your measurements for the case, and a line drawing of the case. You'll need to buy wood, nails, paint, and a brush. You'll also need a hammer and hand drill. If you don't have tools, borrow them from a buddy. Or you can find out everything you need to know at your local hardware store. Don't hesitate to ask—that's what they're there for! You might take my toolbox tips in the Appendix with you to break the ice.

You can also use this same design for videos, DVDs, and CDs by just adding a shelf in-between. And if you build the case sturdy enough, it can double as a bench.

BACHELOR PAD DO'S & DON'TS

- **Do** buy renters insurance if you don't own your home. Computers, TVs, stereos, furniture, sports equipment, and clothes add up to a lot of money—especially if you have to replace them because of theft or fire.

- **Do** secure any pieces of furniture you pick up secondhand. This is extremely important for entertainment centers and bookcases. Tighten the screws, and replace screws and nails where necessary. The last thing you want is for it all to come tumbling down.

- **Do** consider secondhand electronics. You'll find a lot of stuff for not much cash. I'm amazed by how many people have equipment they've hardly used or just recently bought and need to sell.

- **Don't** turn your entertainment center into a fire hazard. Make sure you use a power strip, and check to see that you aren't overloading circuits. Many fires start by people overloading their electrical sockets, especially in an older buildings or homes.

- **Don't** store your CDs, DVDs, tapes, or albums where the sun reaches them. You invested a lot of money in them, so protect them.

- **Don't** store your records flat, always vertical. It's important that the records don't lean to one side, so add a bookend or books to keep them upright.

- **Don't** put up posters of yourself with or without your shirt on, unless you're a model. Even then, it just isn't a good idea. If you can't stop yourself, then consider putting one up as a joke and using it as a dartboard.

- **Don't** put your speakers against a wall that you share with a neighbor if you live in an apartment or condo.

The only failure is not to try. —GEORGE CLOONEY

BASIC INSTINCT

Remember, there is no right or wrong. Trust your instincts. When you go out to catch a pass, your brain decides how fast to run or just how much you need to slow down in order to meet the ball and catch it. After a while, that becomes instinctual. Trust that same process when it comes to making your space work for you. Objects will begin to catch your eye, and you'll realize, "My TV would fit in there." You'll start to see in a different way. Everything you look at will have the possibility to be more than it is.

For instance, you might be looking for a table and chairs, so you drive past a garage sale. You don't see the things you're looking for, but you do see this beat-up laminate bookcase, falling over on its side. All of a sudden, you see it differently—the perfect entertainment center! You envision it on its side, the back panel of the case removed to create four open sections. You cut two small shelves and then add them horizontally in two of the open sections for more display space, and then you paint it a really cool shade of gun-metal gray. You put it on casters and make it mobile.

Some of my leanest years made me dig deep and depend on every creative bone in my body. Get to know what you're made of—see your possibilities

PIPEDREAM

If you want to create a casual atmosphere, say goodbye to the typical twin candlesticks in conventional holders. Think plumbing—as in pipes from your local home-improvement center! With a simple twist of a wrist and a few ordinary galvanized pipes and flanges, you can literally make a set of candlesticks in no time flat.

Head to the plumbing department of your favorite hardware store and look for galvanized plumbing parts. They have all sizes from small to tall.

For every nipple pipe you choose, you need two flanges with the appropriate size to match the ends of the pipes.

It's that simple. Use several different heights and widths, and you can create the perfect atmosphere to pipe some life into your place!

and don't be afraid to try something. It's part of the process. Besides, you'll figure out what you need, when you need it. I promise you that you can't disappoint yourself if you at least *try*!

CLUTTER BUSTERS

- A wall unit is not only aesthetically pleasing but great for storing books, trophies, and sports equipment. If you're into the urban look, get one of those steel racks used to store items in garages. Stashing stuff in metal boxes is another great clutter buster. You can easily paint the metal boxes to match your color scheme.

- Store all the various kinds of remotes in a great looking box; the box keeps them off the coffee table and contains the clutter.

- Return all the metal hangers you get from the dry cleaners and get the same type of hanger, whether it's wood or clear plastic. You will definitely notice the difference!

- Instead of leaving your shoes on the floor, get a shoe holder. Whether its one that hangs in your closet or sits on the closet floor, it will help organize the mess (and you won't have to dig through the pile to find a matching pair later!).

- Make your bed in the morning—no ifs, no ands, no buts, no exceptions. There is nothing more comforting than to come home to a tidy bed.

- Baskets are a great decorative way to declutter. If you have items that are near and dear to you but don't necessarily want them out for all to see, place them in baskets and stack the baskets in a corner or under a table for a fun and efficient look.

- Remember, clutter control is all about keeping the things that are important to you but using the space that you have efficiently. Your pad can still be organized without losing a sense of comfort.

BE A GOOD SPORT

Since you were a boy, sports of every kind have been drilled into your head. The second I gave birth to my son Michael, he had his first baseball glove, infant uniform, Nerf football, and baby-sized sports caps. Mike couldn't walk or talk yet, but he was already set up—destined to be a diehard fan.

Once you go through that growing-up process of learning which sports you love to play, collecting all that equipment, rooting for your team no matter what, and collecting your share of trophies and awards, sports are even more significant.

So what happens with all those trophies? When placed properly, they can look wonderful. We should all have a little corner of pride in our homes. The key is that the older you get, the less prominently those trophies should be featured. They add ambiance to an office or den—as long as you display them in a cool way, and that means framing and placing them in an attractive grouping.

As for the sports equipment that you genuinely use, I have some thoughts and tips on how to display them in an interesting way and still be able to grab them on a moment's notice for that impromptu game. Even if you can't part with those old hockey sticks or baseball bats, here's how to keep them around by swinging them into a different kind of action.

Kayak or Rowboat

A boat can be tricky to store, especially when you have no garage or storage space. If you need to get it down frequently, consider making the boat part of your motif. You'll find wall mounts for storage at any sporting goods store. With a little bit of imagination, your living space can become the Great Outdoors. Try mounting the brackets on the wall over your sofa, and your boat becomes a piece of art! Or mount the brackets on the ceiling—just make sure you have enough space for everyone to walk beneath the boat without ducking.

Add a large tin or ceramic container to hold the oars with some curly willow, like an arrangement, in a corner of the room. You could also display small pine trees in wooden containers and use plaid blankets for accessories. Your coffee table could be out of wood crates. Use your imagination and really have fun with this.

Skis or Snowboards

Your winter gear can also be hung on walls using brackets. Long and thin, skis or snowboards fit into your home much easier than most gear. Hallways are perfect. Include photos of you skiing down the slopes and posters from your favorite ski resorts. Arrange them with your equipment on the hallway walls for an exciting, adventurous passageway.

Play Ball!

Make balls part of the display on your bookshelf or entertainment center. If they look like they were placed there on purpose, then they were—and they become part of the design. Old trunks also work great in living rooms as coffee tables that can double as equipment storage. Baseballs, hockey pucks, handballs, and tennis balls look great in a wooden bowl on your coffee table. You can also include a catcher's mitt as part of the display.

Catcher's or Goalie's Mask

Masks become a great art accessory for the wall. Hang them like you would a collection of tribal or Mardi Gras masks.

Bats, Sticks, Clubs, and Racquets

Old bats, hockey sticks, or tennis racquets can become a sports picture frame. Select a picture or poster to be framed. Use quarter-inch plywood for the back. Have a piece of plexiglas cut to size, and screw the plywood, picture and plexiglas together. Screw a piece of sports equipment to all four sides of the picture on the front. Try baseball bats sliced down the middle into two parts with a jigsaw, as well as tennis racquets, golf clubs, and hockey sticks.

Or turn your collection of bats into a unique wall hanging by placing bookshelf brackets with adjustable L pegs. Place the bats one at a time on the rack like you would position a shelf.

Add a sporting touch to your windows by mounting bats or hockey sticks, even fishing poles, as drapery rods. Pick up inexpensive drapes at linen stores. Just make sure they have big enough openings at the top of the curtain so they'll hang properly on your sporty new drapery rod.

Memorable Game Tickets

When you have tickets from important, memorable sporting events in your life, pick up inexpensive frames in black or leather, and pre-cut mats. Arrange the tickets in one large frame or in several small frames. It's a wonderful inexpensive way to have a special piece of art.

This also makes a neat gift. If you plan ahead, you can take a picture of the person the gift is intended for at the game or function. Frame the picture and the tickets together for an easy, awesome gift. Programs from the event work well also.

Jerseys

Do you have a signed jersey you want to display? If you don't want to pay for the pre-made display box frames, make your own. Build a simple 4-

sided box frame out of lumber. Add a back panel, and enclose the box with plexiglas.

A framing store can cut the plexiglas to the size you need. The wood is up to you, but if you paint the frame, you can go cheap on lumber. Let the home-improvement store cut the wood to your exact specifications.

Memorabilia

If you have collections of memorabilia, highlight them for a dramatic effect. Place them on special shelves, on pedestals, in a case, or in their own entire memorabilia showcase room. Then light them with halogen track lighting in black. It's cheap and easy to install, and you can get extra lights to add as many as you need. Place individual lights on special pieces.

Backboards and Nets

Install an old basketball net over your washer in your laundry room, and jump shot your socks and underwear into the wash!

Turn a backboard or goalie's net into a headboard—if not for you, then maybe a guest or your child's room. It's the perfect size for the sports fan with a twin bed.

SPORTS THEME DO'S AND DON'TS

Do take special care of any sports memorabilia that you would like to pack away for safekeeping (letter sweaters, uniforms, caps, etc.). Clean them first; then store them in a container with cedar sweater bag inserts. The cedar will protect the natural fibers from any insects.

Do deodorize your sports equipment. Febreeze™ works great when you're in a hurry; buy it at any grocery store.

Do use your imagination when decorating with a sports theme. Think about all the ways you can carry a look throughout the room—use a pen stripe that matches a baseball uniform for your drapes, bedding, or couch pillows. Or paint your walls the colors of your team.

Do use good taste and good sense when deciding how far to take your sports theme. Remember that you may also want to transform your space into something romantic once in a while.

Don't hang a sweaty, dirty jersey on your wall. Clean it, or you'll be wondering where the foul odor is coming from. If you're worried about damaging the jersey, have it dry cleaned. Clean any equipment that you're using as a permanent fixture.

PAD POINTS

- Keep it clean! No one wants to come into a dirty home. Pick up the clothes, put down the toilet seat, and make sure the dishes are in the washer.

- Use dimmer switches. Or turn off the lights and light a few candles. Choose masculine scents such as tobacco or bergamot.

- Soften the sofa. Discount stores are a great place to find pillows and throws for a steal. Use masculine colors (rich browns, earthy greens, rusty oranges, slate grays) and comfortable fabrics (cashmere, cotton, leather, linen, suede, and satin). Cuddle up in cashmere, and create a cozy place to relax.

- Freshen up your space with flowers for a special occasion.

- Let the music play. Need I say more? Every great bachelor has "his song." Make that mood magic work for you.

- Collect art. Even if it's a painting that you've done or a photo that you've had enlarged, art is a chic and simple way to ramp up the style factor of a space.

CAFÉ CHIC (BUT BETTER)

For that night with someone special, transform your space into a simple sophisticated setting reminiscent of a European café, stylish and romantic.

If you don't have a dining room, move your kitchen table into the living room and cover it with a white tablecloth. If you don't have a tablecloth, just use a (clean) plain white sheet and tuck the corners under.

Place a few candles (preferably unscented when you're serving food) on the table, and serve your meal with a bottle of wine. Anything goes, simple pasta and salad, or even an easy pizza! Put some music on in the background, and you're good to go.

If the weather is too good to be true, and you have a porch, patio, or backyard, consider moving your table outside. Even if it's at the last minute, your guest is sure to be impressed with your extra effort.

PRESTO PESTO

Cook-free cooking—who doesn't like the sound of that? Here's an easy, no-cook hors d'oeuvre that will make you seem like a gourmet chef.

Equipment

food processor
serving dish or bowl
platter
decorative serving spoon

Shopping List

2 cups fresh basil leaves
⅓ cup pine nuts (chopped walnuts work, too)
3 garlic cloves, minced or finely chopped
½ cup extra virgin olive oil (remember: "light" olive oil does not mean fewer calories; it means less taste!)
½ cup freshly grated Parmesan or Romano cheese (or ¼ cup of each)
Salt and fresh-ground pepper
Pre-cooked pizza dough rounds (I use Boboli)
Fresh Italian bread (sliced)

In a food processor, combine the basil and nuts. Pulse until a paste forms. Add the garlic. Pulse some more. Slowly add the olive oil, with the food processor on. Stop the food processor, and scrape the sides with a rubber spatula (a fork will do, too). Add the grated cheese, and pulse again until blended. The finished consistency of pesto is thick but fairly smooth. Add a pinch of salt and black pepper to taste.

Place the pesto in the bowl, and set the bowl in the middle of your platter. Arrange the pizza rounds and the sliced Italian bread around the bowl of pesto and serve! Also, consider tossing on a sprig of red grapes if you have them handy, or a chunk of Parmesan cheese for presentation.

And there you have it. *Presto pesto!*

OPEN UP

Yes, you're a bachelor, but most important, you're a *dad*! Staying involved with your children is essential to their well-being and development. Whether making a meal together (or just eating it), playing hide-n-seek in the back yard, or even making a simple phone call, spending time with your kids is vital.

Your role in your children's life is just as important as the mother's. Studies show that the usual rough-and-tumble of dad play teaches children how to manage emotions, such as excitement. Kids with active fathers are generally more popular and socially secure. So get out there and be active, not just for your sake, but for their sake, too!

As important as roughhousing is, it is equally important for you to be emotionally available to your kids. Learn to listen to your feelings so that you can learn to better listen to theirs.

More than anything, your kids just want to talk with you. They want you to know who they are and to share their ups and downs with you. Have a routine with your children where you set aside time just to be together. A hike, an art project, reading a book, playing a sport—even just an email—time spent with your children is critical.

ROAD WEARY KIDS

It's important to create a special place in your home that really makes children feel welcome. It's usually difficult enough for children traveling "between homes" to deal with the emotions that go along with a nontraditional household. So take extra care when creating a space for children who might naturally feel a bit "homeless." Find ways to make them always feel like they are coming home when they walk through the front door. Let them select the bedding and color of the space. Allow them to bring photos so that they feel as though some of their home life is with them. Keep the parent relationships in mind! It is extremely important for them to be allowed to have a photo of Mom or Dad in their room, if that's what they need. They might want to have special pajamas and toiletries waiting. That way the packing is left to a minimum and they take ownership of their room. Soon they will begin to look forward to their home away from home.

RUG-GEDLY HANDSOME

Area rugs make it easy and inexpensive to add color, warmth, and style to a bare floor. They can change the look of any room. So don't neglect the floors of your rooms!

Floors are great palettes for pattern, color, and texture. An area rug can set the tone or even become the focal point of a room, depending on the colors, pattern, and shape you choose.

You could use accent rugs to define smaller areas in a larger room, like separating a conversation area from a recreation area. Rugs are perfect for making large rooms seem more intimate by using color and texture for definition.

And believe it or not, large area rugs don't have to cost a fortune. Here's one way to create an area rug from a few simple bath mats. It's easy on the eye and the pocketbook!

1 Measure your floor space to determine the maximum and minimum area. (I used six 2- by 3-foot bathroom mats for mine.)

2 Look for bath mats that have a little texture to them, like cotton shag. Be sure the mats have squared-off corners. (Don't be afraid of bright colors!)

3 Use painter's tape to flatten down the shag and make a clear path for sewing. Painter's tape works well because it won't tear out any material when you remove it.

4 Sew the mats together by hand using upholstery needles and strong upholstery thread. Since you're sewing through a thick mat, use a thimble.

And there you have it! A new, custom area rug that looks like a special order straight from a rug gallery. It's so easy to make and adds so much to your living room.

Shopping List

Several 2- by 3-foot bath mats
Measuring tape
Sharp scissors
Matching upholstery thread
Upholstery needles (buy at any knit shop or hardware store)
Thimble
Painter's tape

I think everyone should have a healthy perspective about awards. Awards represent an accomplishment, an appreciation for your talent and incredible hard work. You should enjoy them and have a sense of humor about it!

If you have wall plaques and certificates and aren't sure how to hang them without putting a zillion holes in the wall, here's an absolutely foolproof tip:

1. Trace each framed certificate or plaque that you want to hang onto drawing paper or newspaper. Cut out each template.

2. Arrange the templates onto the wall with pins or tape.

3. On each actual picture or plaque, measure from the tip of the wire's arc to the top of the frame. On the matching template, measure in from the top edge this same distance to mark where the picture hook should meet the wire hanger on the wall.

4. Nail the picture hook onto the template, so that the bottom of the hook is on the mark. Rip the paper right off the wall, leaving the hooks perfectly placed.

5. Hang your Wall of Fame. Life is short, so celebrate who you are!

FLOWERLESS FLOWER ARRANGING

If fruits and flowers aren't your thing, you can still bring in a sense of the organic. Consider arrangements presented in thick glass cylinders (round or square) filled with river rocks, curly willow, or sand.

If you like the idea of an arrangement of wood but want to spice it up a bit, spray-paint your curly willow (or twigs from the yard, even). Pick something bright and vibrant like rusty orange or turquoise, or go neutral with matte white or pewter.

Bachelor basics

Name the top three things that you love about being a bachelor. Then name the top three things you don't so much love about it.

Are the things you don't love evident in your home? What are they, and how do these things affect your life?

What is your passion—sports, music, movies? Is your passion taking over your home or hiding somewhere inside?

What can you do to find the right balance?

Do you have a sense of your personal style? If so, what is it? Does your home reflect this style?

Challenge yourself to spend money on small luxuries—600-thread-count sheets or nice scented candles.

Make a list of a few items you'd be willing to splurge on for a touch of luxury in your home.

I laugh when people tell me they're afraid to have me over to their homes! I'm shocked they think I'm actually coming over to investigate how they are living. For years, Martha Stewart did some really funny guest spots on television sitcoms spoofing herself—the skits involved people inviting her for a dinner or a party and coming unglued by their own fear of perfection. Life is not about perfection, so why should entertaining be? Get those old "rules of entertaining" out of your head! Kick back, relax, and be the life of the party!

life of the PARTY

The most important message of this book is to encourage you to give up any fear of not being perfect by embracing a new way of thinking. I understand anyone's anxiety because I have experienced it, but entertaining doesn't have to be difficult or stressful. You don't have to raise the grain-fed chicken you're serving for dinner, wring its neck, and pluck it in order to say you made the dinner from scratch. You don't even need to roast that chicken yourself if you don't want to! Simply pick one up already cooked if you like. What's important is to spend your time relaxing and rejuvenating yourself, and spending time with your friends or family.

When your friends come over for a dinner party, they want to see and visit with *you.* If you spend the entire evening in the kitchen, then you defeat the reason for having them over in the first place. So let go, and enjoy yourself!

I love to cook and prepare my husband's favorite meals. And when my son Michael visits, I'm definitely going to cook for him! But when life is *normal*— crazy with work, appointments, sporting events, and every kind of lessons for our children imaginable—then we just have to figure out a better way! So if your schedule won't allow time to chop and sauté, find another path. (In my home, we call it "The Anderson Way"—you get the idea.)

That's the secret of entertaining. You make your guests feel welcome and at home. If you do that honestly, the rest takes care of itself. —BARBARA HALL

life of the PARTY

Whether it's Chinese takeout or the Thanksgiving turkey, the key to serving any meal is *presentation*. Serve your meal on that hardly used good china you've been saving! While there is definitely a place in the world for paper plates, I'm saying this: Dust off that china and wipe the year-old fingerprints off your crystal, and make them part of your everyday life. *You* are the special guest, and you deserve to treat *yourself*. You'll be amazed how special you feel when you enjoy your diet soda or milk from a beautiful glass. Use everything you have!

So throw out that old thinking handed down from generation to generation. Let go of socially imposed performance anxiety. Oh yes, you can pull off an elegant dinner party! Turn entertaining into something fun, and you'll do it more often.

But also keep in mind that presentation isn't all that matters. Recently, I realized I haven't been able to see my friends as much as I would like. I decided it was more important to spend time together in any way possible than to try to create the "ultimate" dining experience. So every now and then, we just order takeout and hang. Shooting the breeze is seriously underrated. No dishes, no mess—it's just about being together in our homes. When I have time, I still entertain with an elaborate dinner party because I enjoy it. Opening our homes is a gift that we share with those we love. But we don't have to make excuses or try to impress each other. We're just happy to share time together. You will be, too.

Moll

My best buddy Karen Hall and I had breakfast together almost every morning for about two years when I lived in Phoenix, Arizona. One morning Karen announced that she was going to give her parents a 50th anniversary party.

If you knew Karen, you would know that this would be very stressful and would dominate everything until the big day! Of course, I swore to be by her side planning and plotting every single step. Arizona weather is pretty amazing, so we decided it should be outside.

The day finally arrived and it started to sprinkle and then rain! Karen's home really wasn't large enough to house all the guests. There was only one possible place we could move this party at the last minute. Karen's husband John, a photographer, had a cool studio. The only problem was that the decor was definitely minimal. It would take putting up a lot of stuff to create an environment that would scream "Happy Anniversary."

I ran home and grabbed every candelabra that I owned, pillows, and throws. I also grabbed some large bolts of fabric that I wasn't using and threw them in the back of the SUV. We hung the fabric in the plain guest bath and made it look as though it had drapes—we turned it into an amazing powder room simply by hammering a few small nails. We transformed that studio with what we had between us. And the party was a huge success!

Usually throwing a cocktail or dinner party takes weeks of advanced preparation—if you're caught up in the perfection mindset! But a get-together is meant to be just that—getting together! So forget all the nitty-gritty details if what you really want to do is bring together people you enjoy spending time with. Don't let the preparation consume you; there are easy, cost-effective ways to throw an amazing party that only *looks* like it took long hours and a lot of money to put together. Use just three of my favorite things: music, lighting, and flowers!

If you've already started living a sense-inspired life, then you're much closer to "party ready" than you might know. If music, lighting, and flowers are a part of your daily life, just think about how easy it will be to transform your space into a place that is ready for entertaining at the last minute.

Pump Up the Tunes!

Most party countdowns say to start playing music 20 minutes before the guests arrive. But why wait? Play music to get you in the mood and keep you entertained as you're getting ready to entertain. If you have a specific mix or soundtrack that you think fits the mood of your get-together, play that while you get ready. It sets the ambiance while you set the stage. And take at least 10 minutes for yourself before your guests arrive. Just sit and relax, and take it all in.

Let There Be Light!

Light is one of the easiest things we can change to really affect the mood of any space. Maybe it's subconscious childhood birthday memories coming through, or perhaps the fact that we rarely remember to treat ourselves with such a simple solution, but everyone seems to love candles! Just the act of lighting some candles around the room will make your guests feel special and welcome. If you're having a small dinner party, dim the overheads and light your candles to create an intensely intimate environment. If you're having a brunch, think natural lighting, but a few candles will add that special spark to your gathering!

Substitute Blooms!

Flowers are such an easy way to liven up a space. It's great if you can run to your local florist or the grocery store to get fresh flowers for your event, but if time is tight, think of the things around your house that could work in place of the traditional arrangement. Try bright fall leaves in red and orange scattered down the center of the table, or fill several clear glass bowls with lemons and limes. Another great party-ready timesaver are year-round dried or silk arrangements. At the very last minute, toss in something you have around the house—pomegranates for fall, twigs or berries for winter, green apples for spring!

PARTY READY?

Okay, here's a test: Pretend you just got a call from six of your friends, and they're 30 minutes away. Can you throw a party based on what you have in your home *right now*? No cheating. This isn't a "Well, it would take me only 20 minutes to run to the store" situation.

See what you *really* have, and see that you *don't* need to hire professional cleaners, caterers, and decorators to throw an amazing get-together—even at the last minute! It's all there; you just need to dig!

Look around your house: What's in the fridge and the cabinets? Do you have some cute cocktail napkins? Some candles and music to set the mood? Take what you've learned from this chapter and create a last-minute party using what you already have around!

Make a list of the things that you come up with. That way, the next time a friend calls, you'll be confident to know that you're party ready.

MINI-TIME, MEGA BITE

Just because it's a dinner party, that doesn't mean you have to *cook dinner*. Here are some simple (and virtually cooking-free) last-minute menus that are sure to please your guests and fit your timeframe.

Backyard BBQ (even without the grill)

Go with traditional American outdoor favorites such as barbeque chicken, baked beans, corn on the cob, and ice cream. If you have the grill, go for it, but if it doesn't fit your budget or the space, use rotisserie chicken from the grocery store and smother it with your favorite BBQ sauce. If you can have a BBQ without the grill, why can't you have it without the sauce? Give your guests several options for their chicken dipping pleasure. Baked beans come in a can, and are easily left to warm on their own. Just be sure to give it an extra kick with your own spices, herbs, and fresh ingredients. Corn on the cob is a given in the summer and ready in just minutes. And ice cream—well, that speaks for itself. If you have the time, make-your-own sundae bars are great; otherwise, save yourself the hassle and the mess, and serve your guests individually packaged ice cream bars.

Sunday Brunch

Choose fresh berries, waffles, pancakes, and mimosas! Pick up a carton of strawberries, raspberries, and blueberries from the grocery, and while you're at it, a tub of whipped cream! Dump the berries into a strainer and run them under cool water. Place the whipped cream in a pretty bowl and serve it alongside the berries. Pancakes are best when they're straight from the griddle (go with prepared mixes), but you'll find some tasty toaster waffles out there too! And who could ask for an easier drink than mimosas? Leave the orange juice and champagne separate, and let guests pour their own concoctions!

Last-Minute Dinner Party

If you have no time to shop, try "toss-it-in" dishes. Start with a basic pasta or salad, and turn up the wow factor with just a few party-ready ingredients like olives, fresh Parmesan cheese, and sun-dried tomatoes. They'll turn the blandest of bases into the most fabulous of finishes.

When making a salad, don't get stuck in the vegetable garden. Think about fruits and nuts, too. A few dried cranberries, a chopped apple, or diced pineapple really make a statement! Just "toss it in"—and turn ordinary to outstanding in seconds.

STOCK OPTIONS

In order to help you be party ready at a moment's notice, keep these must-have pantry staples in stock.

Assorted olives—They have a long shelf life yet seem exotic and decadent. You'll find great varieties, and olives are wonderful stuffed with such delicacies as jalapeños and blue cheese.

Seedless grapes—Not only are they tasty, but they're the perfect garnish for cheese platters and salty hors d'oeuvres.

Frozen finger foods—Discount stores or groceries often have amazing frozen appetizers. Get a box of assorted munchies, and store them for emergencies. Just thaw, garnish, and look gourmet!

Various cheeses—Cheeses are such a treat and a very chic party-ready purchase. A cheese platter makes you and your guests feel special.

Cocktail napkins—Cute or cool cocktail napkins can save the day. If you don't have them, don't distress. But if you have them on hand, they bring a touch of class to any last-minute gathering.

Lemons and limes—Zest with the best! Lemons and limes are such versatile stock. Everything from cocktail garnish to a simple centerpiece, these citrus savers are a party-ready must.

BEVERAGE BASICS

- Invest in a set of all-purpose 11-ounce stemware. They can be used for anything in a pinch (white wine, red wine, champagne, mixed drinks, and non-alcoholic bubblies)! I also love the new stemless wineglass that has emerged over the last few years. It not only has a great look, but is more functional—it's less likely to tip.

- Also have a set (four to six, at least) each of highball and on-the-rocks glasses. Spend the extra money on a nice set of barware, and use them as everyday glasses, as well.

- Even if you don't drink alcoholic beverages, it's nice to have a few basics to offer to a guest. Staples include red and white wines, vodka, whiskey, and beer. Keep in mind that the "drink by" date on beer is more a marketing scheme than a health warning. The flavor may change a bit, but beer doesn't really "go bad" unless you keep it forever. So go ahead and keep a six-pack in the fridge. But if you do refrigerate it, keep it refrigerated or it will go bad (as will champagne).

1-800-GOURMET-PIZZA

Delivery pizza is the time-crunch staple for many Americans. Here's an easy way to give this last-minute meal a gourmet touch.

When ordering a pizza for a last-minute dinner, go for the thin crust and keep it simple. Once the pizza arrives, put it on a cookie sheet and preheat your oven to broil. Drizzle some extra virgin olive oil over the top of the pizza. Push a clove of fresh garlic through your garlic press, and sprinkle it on top. Add a little salt and some fresh-ground pepper. Always keep fresh basil handy; tear the leaves and toss those on top of the pizza, too. Consider adding chopped artichoke hearts, pitted kalamata olives, and feta cheese. Broil for just a few minutes. Don't look away—you'll burn it if you do! Anything that you love on pizza goes; the fresh ingredients are what make it special. Serve with a salad, and you've made this staple a little more special. Tip: Italian dressing (I like Good Seasons brand) mixed with balsamic vinegar and olive oil is fantastic for your salad dressing.

ROASTED CHICKEN FETTUCCINI *the Anderson way*

Shopping List

1 roasted chicken from the grocery store (yes, already cooked)

1 package frozen peas

1 container sliced fresh mushrooms

1 package alfredo white cream sauce mix (I like Schillings)

1 package fresh fettuccini

1 container really good grated Parmesan cheese

1 package fresh basil

Salt and pepper

Fresh garlic

Olive oil

Butter

Debone the roasted chicken. I like to pull it off the bone by hand. If it's a good roasted chicken, the meat will just fall off the bone. Set the chicken in a bowl until needed.

In a saucepan, prepare the alfredo cream sauce according to the directions on the package. (I use real cream instead of milk and butter.) Set aside. If you're dieting, you can use low-fat milk, and if you're lactose intolerant, try a dairy substitute.

Bring water for the pasta to a boil, adding just a dash of salt and about a tablespoon of olive oil.

In a heated skillet, add a dab of butter and quickly sauté the mushrooms. Throw in the frozen peas. Toss in the chicken, and add a tablespoon of olive oil. Heat thoroughly. Add fresh garlic, and salt and pepper to taste.

Add the sauce to the chicken, mushrooms, and peas. Turn the heat to low.

Cook the fresh pasta. Don't overcook—make sure it's *al dente* (a little chewy "to the teeth" is perfect). Drain.

Place the pasta on a plate, and top it off with the chicken and sauce. Toss a sprig of fresh basil on top, and *Buon Appetito!*

PROJECT: PARTY

Step One

Plan your dream party. If you could plan the perfect party (even if just in your mind), what would it be? Who would be on the guest list? What would you serve? What location would it be in? What music would set the scene? Go all out! Be decadent; be fun!

Plan your party before you continue reading...

Step Two

Now actually do it! What do you already have that you can use to throw your dream party? Say that you want to throw a Parisian-inspired soirée under the Eiffel Tower; then consider stringing white lights around your apartment or backyard. Create a wine and cheese bar (even if it's just wine from a box and cheddar!). Think big and think wow—and then think "Oh! I've got that already!"

PARTY-READY DRESSING DO'S & DON'TS

A little prep work at your leisure makes you party ready all the time!

Do choose what you're wearing the night before. The key is to have a couple of comfortable outfits (other than jeans) that you can count on so that if it *is* last minute, you've always got a choice handy.

Do keep a lipstick and compact handy in your kitchen drawer for a little touch up.

Don't wear high heels; be comfortable.

Don't wear long sleeves that hang into the food you're preparing.

Don't let your hair hang long—it might end up in the food. The quickest fix for long hair is a ponytail or an up-do! You don't want to have to think about your hair all night.

Don't wait until the last minute to take a shower or put on your makeup. Do both about one hour before your guests are to arrive. You want to be available when your guests are at your door.

USE WHAT YOU HAVE!

Think outside the box, and work with what you have! Whatever you make your guests perceive to be special will be special. You just have to get it out of your mind that entertaining has to be a "certain way"—think beyond the basics. Working with what you have just isn't a rule for entertaining and the home; it's a rule for life too!

- If you don't have votives, try small glasses and drop tea-lights in them!

- If you don't have special party-music compilations, put on a soundtrack to fit the mood.

- If you don't have dimmers, just turn the lights off and light the candles. Or lay a colorful scarf over your lampshade to add a bit of drama and ambiance.

- If you don't have a centerpiece, there's good news: you don't need one! Consider an individual arrangement for each place, or pull from the fridge or yard (artichokes, lemons, leaves, or branches—anything goes!).

- If you don't have the makings of a meal, order pizza and use my easy pizza pepper-upper to spruce it up with what you have (olive oil, crushed red pepper, basil leaves—whatever you like)!

ICE-BREAKER

A dear friend of mine always asks that I email her in advance with the names and a little background on each guest attending any gathering she'll also be at. I have adopted this hostess trick as my own, no matter the occasion. The next time you're throwing a party, treat your guests to a little insider information, and give them a chance to get to know one another even before the big day.

There's nothing like a theme to get guests excited about a party! It's an experience that allows us to step outside our everyday schedules and mix fantasy with friends. Theme parties are also great ice-breakers, giving guests an immediate connection to each other. Once you've decided your theme, start with what is easily available; anything that you can get locally makes your life easier.

The Web is a fabulous tool for any party planner. Just type in a few words with your theme subject, and literally hundreds of related ideas or possibilities pop up to assist you. With overnight shipping options, you can get just about anything the next day. Here's one theme party planned for you!

The Best Darn Takeout Party Outside The Orient!

To have as much fun as possible without the stress, order takeout from your favorite Chinese or other Asian restaurant. Choose colors for your theme—red and black are very powerful and traditional with this Asian motif. Add "Asian Attire" to your invitation if you like, or simply ask your guests to come dressed in either of the party colors.

Spice up your space with some Asian flair, and make your dinner a Shanghai success. Everything is optional—add more or less and have a fabulous time either way.

Shopping List

Chop sticks
Chinese fans
Chinese lanterns
Candles
Throw pillows with Asian motifs
Rice bowls
Sake cups
Chinese teapot
Square plates
Sake
Chinese tea
Fortune cookies
Soy sauce
Chinese hot sauce

Never let your guests leave without some little remembrance of the evening they've experienced. Here are two simple ideas.

Personalized Fortune Cookies

Buy traditional fortune cookies; then remove the original fortunes with tweezers.

Measure the original fortune, and cut blank pieces of white paper to the same size.

Write a personalized fortune for each guest and slip the fortune back into the cookie. Place the personalized fortune cookie at their seat.

Sake to You

Create a sake set for each couple or guest.

Place the shredded red paper into the (bamboo) basket and then arrange the sake set so it is displayed in the basket. Place the opened fan at an angle and then position the chop sticks so they are sticking out of the basket. You can arrange in many possible ways; be creative. The idea is to get the sake set out of its original box and create it a special take-away gift. Tie on your personalized card, and then sake to them!

Shopping List (for each set)

Sake set
1 bag of shredded red paper
1 Chinese fan
2 sets of chop sticks
1 basket or container to hold the
sake set (try bamboo)
1 small personalized note card to
attach to the gift

Party all the time

Describe the most memorable party you've ever attended. What was it about the party that made it so special to you?

What was the most disastrous party you've attended, and what went wrong?

_____

_____

_____

_____

_____

_____

_____

_____

_____

Write about what you think your friends say about your entertaining abilities. Do you entertain like your mother? Are you too anxious? Too high-stress? Too relaxed? (I don't really think that last one's possible, but this is about what you think.)

_____

_____

_____

_____

_____

_____

_____

_____

_____

_____

How do you feel 24 hours before a party and then the morning after?

Plan a party on a budget using tips that you've learned in this chapter. Name your party essentials (what do you just have to have), and then hunt around your home to come up with fun (inexpensive) décor and food items that fit your theme!

SPECIAL TOUCHES: ROOM BY ROOM

Just as extra thick towels and a feather duvet can make a hotel room something more than just a place to spend the night, a few special touches can transform a simply functional room into something luxurious. Try some of these ideas:

Living Room

- Use a soft throw blanket.
- Dim the lights and light candles.
- Rearrange your art.
- Turn off the TV, and just play music.

Kitchen

- Keep hand lotion by the sink—and use it.
- Put lemon in your water (also try mint!).
- Stock fresh basil in the fridge; it adds so much flavor to many dishes.
- Hide or disguise your trashcan.
- Display a bowl of fresh lemons or limes.

Bathroom

- Keep toiletries tucked away in baskets.
- Display pretty containers of bath salts.
- Enjoy a bath surrounded by candles.
- Use hand soap that you love the smell of.
- Fold your towels in a new way—roll and place them in a cool basket, or stack them neatly on a bench.
- Put fresh flowers by the sink.

Kid's Room

- Frame and hang your child's art.
- Use comfy sheets in the kid's room, too.
- Go wild with paint on a wall or piece of furniture (try chalk paint).
- Always have books!

Nursery

- Install a dimmer switch.
- Sing a song or play music.
- Include a comfortable chair and a soft blanket.
- Keep the baby supplies tucked away in baskets.
- Stay simple. Don't clutter with too many stuffed animals or go overboard with themes.

Dining Room

- Have family dinners at least twice a week (every night if possible).
- Use the nice china.
- Dim the lights, and light candles with your meals.

Home Office

- Play music to motivate and soothe, not distract.
- Keep all supplies neatly organized and tucked away.
- Hang a framed quote by the desk or over the door.

Garage

- Hang curtains over storage shelves to hide the junk.
- Paint the walls (even the floor) a fun color.
- Hang art! It's the first thing you see every time you come enter the garage.
- Get a doormat that you love.
- If you have the space, try fake foliage such as a large palm or a flower arrangement.

Bedroom

Here are a few tips to keep you from waking up on the wrong side of your bed:

- Determine your budget, but remember that the first thing on your list has to be a great mattress.

- Enjoy the luxury of excellent sheets. Get the highest thread count you can afford—at least 400-thread count. (No poly-blends!)

- Choose a color that reflects the vibe you want; paint the room into something that you feel inspired by or drawn to.

- Think clean and sleek lines. Our rooms need not be full of furniture to be fabulous. A Zen room with a simple bed on a platform, a large vase with curly willow, and a couple of pillows might be just the place to bring you calm and comfort.

- Save the family photos for the family room. Photos of parents tend to quash the romance! Choose art that evokes the mood you desire.

- Don't buy a matching set of bedroom furniture. Mixing is so much more sophisticated and interesting.

- Keep your bedroom clean and neat. Use baskets or boxes with lids to house all the junk.

- Make your bed in the morning. Fluff your pillows.

- Remember that you are always the most important person to enter your bedroom. Every now and then, give yourself "the walk-in test"—look at the room as though you are seeing it for the first time.

Love the One You're With

If your bathroom tile is deco style and pink, don't despair—and don't paint your walls a color that will only make it worse, like cobalt blue or gold (trust me; I've seen them!). Choose a color to make that room more sophisticated. Black (or even chocolate brown) is always a lifesaver in the style department.

If you have your grandmother's matching bedroom set, headboard, end tables, dresser, and mirror, be grateful! But be willing to paint the headboard or antique it for a fresh new look. Move the end tables into a guest bedroom. Use your dresser as a buffet in your dining room or as an entry piece with the mirror painted for an elegant vibe. Mix things up!

If your walls are old plaster and beat up, embrace them! Give them an old world vibe. Go ahead and beat them up a bit more. Use a rag to paint on three colors. It's an amazing look.

Draperies add softness and cover a multitude of sins, such as a window opening to a poor view. To heighten ceilings, hang drapes as high as possible. If you don't want to invest in custom, then drape the fabric generously over inexpensive rods.

Does your mantel need a lift? Consider antiquing it! Use an oil-based glaze, a tint, and a little sandpaper for some aging. It gives the impression that you might have picked it up at an antique shop.

De-stress with distressing. Take any pent-up energy out on the cabinets with a hammer. Then pick up some glaze and some burnt umber paint; mix together and give those newly dented cabinets that well-worn look.

Sort It—Trash It—Store It—Stash It!

Every room can affect your life, but what's the one thing that all rooms generally have in common? Clutter! Clutter can so easily get out of hand and take over your life. I have a simple solution for every room in your home to help keep clutter at bay. This easy 4-step process can take as little or as long as you want.

Sort it!

Locate the source of the clutter. Is it an overflowing closet, a cabinet under the sink, or an entire room? Get to the source, and start to sort!

Trash It!

A lot of clutter is trash. For example, get rid of those old, crusty, mostly empty shampoo bottles. If you just can't part with the product, empty the contents into a smaller travel-sized bottle or a cool dispenser. Repeat with everything in your home. Toss the trash so you can get to the good stuff.

Store It!

Once you've separated trash from treasure, decide what needs to be stored (items you don't use more than once every three months) and what needs to stay (things you use on a daily basis). Store items in clear plastic stackable containers. Label them clearly, and store them label side out. You might also try clear plastic bags. Just keep your containers clear and labeled so you don't have to open each bag or box to see what's there.

Stash It!

When I say stash it, I mean just that! Find a place to put what you need to keep at hand. Baskets are a clever compromise between storage and style. They're the easiest way to organize your items so they're not out on the counter or all over the floor. Just toss your stuff in a basket. You'll find every possible style, size, and material, so use baskets for everything from socks to soaps, tools to toiletries, forks to fruit, paper to paint, anything! Class up your clutter with baskets, and just stash it. Clean the clutter from those baskets at least once every six months!

HOME AWAY FROM HOME

I often find myself literally living out of a suitcase! For a major homebody like me, travel definitely puts my philosophy and lifestyle tips to the maximum test. But I'm happy to say that home is a place you create—and can take with you. So whether you're on the road, at college, or creating a warm environment for guests, you can create a sense of home.

When creating a home-like atmosphere, my five must-haves—paint, lighting, music, flowers, and fabric—are essential and can easily be portable. Whether it's warming up a space with candles (if allowed) and flowers, or setting out photographs of family and friends, staying connected to your home will definitely help you make it through the day. Treat every space in your life like a room in your home.

With just a little bit of planning, you can make the whole experience or space so much better. Wherever your heart and soul is, that's home.

- When I stay in a hotel, I create a comfortable space just for me. I always bring pictures and my own pillow. A candle and fresh flowers are also a must. Spoil yourself—I do! Start your day with room service coffee, fresh blueberries, croissants, and jam. For me, such small luxuries make being away from home tolerable. Create a few rituals that can translate from home to a hotel. If you and your partner like to make breakfast or dinner on the weekend and watch a movie at home, don't give that up. Order room service and pay per view!

- If you're not traveling with your partner or you're away from your children, carry a framed photo or two to set on the nightstand. That way, they'll be the first thing you see when you wake up and the last thing you see before you go to bed.

- Personal communication devices and cell phones with text message features are simple ways to stay in constant touch. It's important to check in nightly and include your family in your experience so you don't feel absent and they feel secure about your safety.

- Many commute to work or travel for business and spend countless days and nights yearning to get to a home base. So whether it's a hotel room, a plane, a camper, tent, or tour bus, take important items and some necessary luxuries to make you feel more at home. Carry a larger bag than usual when you travel. Guys, consider one of the new soft briefcases; they look masculine but function like a small tote.

- Most hotels are happy to arrange to have fresh flowers in your room, but I like to stop at a florist or even a nearby grocery and grab a bunch.

- If you travel often or on short notice, keep two stocked toiletry travel bags, one you always have packed in your suitcases ready to go and one that stays at home. To save time packing, double up on your make-up, as well.

Must-Have Travel Kits

- Small medicine bag with the basics—medicines (over-the-counter and your prescriptions), first-aid cream, and band-aids (liquid band-aids are great for blisters on the feet).

- Small sewing kit—including small scissors and superglue (great for a broken nail).

- Extra phone charger and computer cord—I've left behind countless cords, and apparently, so does everybody else. If you lose your phone or computer cords, check with the hotel. They often keep a box of unclaimed ones.

- Pillow and blanket—my first choice is always cashmere. It's really quite practical, but also very warm and luxurious.

- Candles and a lighter—travel with the same scent you use at home; you'll be amazed how comforting that can be.

The Best for Your Guests

Guests to your home are away from their home, so strive to create a space for guests. Entertaining friends in the home is one of the most intimate gifts we can share. So it's important to add special touches that really make them feel welcome. One of the best (and easiest) places to pamper your guests is in the guest bath. Take a few minutes to set out elegant soaps and rolled towels before dinner guests arrive. If you're expecting overnight company, the bathroom is the perfect place to make them feel welcome. A simple setting of bath salts, a natural sponge, fresh toiletries, and a robe and slippers help to create a sense of homey hospitality.

Be sure your guests feel the comforts of home in your space, too. Provide a few special luxuries to pamper your guests. Just a few quick tricks can help you create a home away from home experience for a visitor at the drop of a hat.

- Candles are an easy way to add a welcoming ambiance to your home. Use seasonal scents and colors to warm up your entryway, living room, or guest bedroom. Just light a few, and you can transform a space from monotonous to mood setting.

- Select some special music to set the scene. Think festive for a large gathering and intimate instrumentals for smaller get-togethers.

- Make your guests feel like they're at a quaint bed and breakfast. Stock their bathroom with a hand towel folded to form a pocket, and stuff it with mini-bottles of lotion, body wash, shampoo, or toothpaste.

- Place a small vase of flowers by your guest's bed or in the bathroom. It's amazing how a simple thing like flowers can freshen up an otherwise drab space.

- If your guest bedroom doubles as a home office or workout area, make sure the clutter is down to a minimum. A cluttered mess is the least inviting way to say come on in!

Dorm Rooms 101

Possibly one of the most challenging spaces to decorate, a dorm room is not only small, but supposed to serve as a fully functional bedroom, living room, office, and kitchen all wrapped up in one! With a roommate! On top of that, there are strict rules about what you can (but mostly cannot) do to the space. How do you make this space feel like home, while still keeping it functional, respecting your roomie, and not breaking the bank?

Personal touches are the key to creating a home away from home. Before you make the big move to college, collect a few of your favorite photographs of friends and family , or pictures of special places. Put them in a collection of similar frames to keep the look cohesive; select sleek silver, rustic wood, leather, or basic black. Consider copying your pictures in black and white or sepia tones (you can enlarge them too!). The pictures will have a unified look—and you'll have a work of art!

- Add drama to your dorm. Just because you're going to move at the end of the semester doesn't mean you can't create a luxurious living environment. One of the easiest ways to add drama is with lighting. Installing a dimmer switch probably isn't in the budget or university guidelines, but you can still get the look of dimmed light by using lots of lamps instead of the harsh fluorescent overheads. (Be mindful of overusing outlets, however.)

- If your room has built-in drawers, change out the knobs to reflect your personal style. Just be sure to save the old ones, so you can replace them at the end of year!

- Can you have a kick of color without getting kicked off campus? Think drapes, bedding, and large area rugs! Using fabric on the windows and floors adds color, but it also brings comfort to the room. An area rug and drapes can soften and frame a space, and make so much difference.

- Purchase inexpensive rods, and hang drapes as high as you possibly can to give the usually low dorm room ceiling the illusion of a bit more height. Then just purchase some simple curtains and hang them! They'll really give bare space a homey quality.

- Cover cold flooring with a plush rug—think shag for funk, Berber for functional, or even sea-grass for an island feel. Keep in mind that a dorm room is an extremely high-traffic area. Try dark colors or disguising patterns. Or take a tip from an eastern tradition and ask that everyone remove shoes before entering. Either way, it's something to consider when picking a carpet.

Dorm Room Solutions

- Figure out how to use every inch of space—bed risers maximize space under your bed that otherwise would be "lost."

- Buy some long plastic storage containers that fit under beds; you can store items that you need but may not use daily.

- Grab some fun-colored acrylic containers and label each. Store them at the edge of your bed and fill them with desk supplies, socks, shoes—you get the idea.

- Maximize the space inside your closet. Buy ready-made shelves at any home-improvement center. Remember, if it has a bare wall—it can hold a shelf!

- Add bookshelves at the foot of your bed.

TOOLBOX BASICS

Home improvement television is a great tool. So many weekend warriors have come out of their shells thanks to the huge variety of television programming. Any day, at any hour, you can surf dozens of programs to find a project or some great advice on exactly what you need. Ours is an amazing time for Do-It-Yourself-ers.

Contractors are a wonderful tool that we in the design world can't live without. They take the brunt of the poor press when it comes to home remodeling. But do your research, and you'll find the very best. Hire a reputable, licensed contractor, and be willing to pay for it. Check out references, and take a walk through some of their work.

Don't overlook one of the most handy tools—the "handy" guy or gal who can fix what needs fixing! Let's face it. Some of us are simply too busy to fix that fence, change out that old chandelier, or fix the toilet. Those handy folk ride in and save the day so easily!

Toolbox Tips

- It's important to take care of your tools, so the first thing you need is a toolbox. You'll find many to choose from that are very reasonable. I like the classic red metal one.

- Buy one tool at a time. A prepackaged set will get you off to a good start, but then you're also buying things that you'll probably never use.

- Always handle a tool first—you need something with a good weight and feel for you.

- Consider tools that have more than one use, like a four-in-one screwdriver.

- Never mind the fancy handles. Focus on function.

- It's important to invest in quality if you want tools to be around a long time. Tools that bend or break will slow you down and might cause damage.

- Keep your tools nice, dry, and tidy—they will last forever.

Toolbox Must-Haves

10-ounce hammer
Four-in-one screwdriver
Long-nose and slip-joint pliers
8-inch adjustable wrench
Utility knife
9-inch level
25-foot extension cord
Flashlights
25-foot tape measure
Colored duct tape
Cordless power drill
(when you can afford one)

Toolbox Nice-to-Haves

Sturdy ladder
Plunger
Assorted sizes of nails
Picture hangers
Work gloves
Superglue
White school glue

Expert Tools of the Trade

Sometimes it is best to just leave it to the professionals. If you or someone in your household isn't quite as "handy" as you thought, I've got some advice on outsourcing the job to a pro rather than spending lots of wasted time (and frustration) doing a botched job.

Surveys show that the average American household has approximately twenty-two items on their to-do list. Rather than wasting time playing phone tag with the plumber, electrician, and carpenter get all your needs met by hiring a professional handyman service.

Tips To Hiring a Handyman Service

- All employees of the company should be prescreened (this includes drug screening and background checks). They also should wear photo identification.

- Don't use a company that subcontracts work. These services often lack consistency and quality control.

- Be sure that your handyman service has insurance and that their workers are bonded.

- Ask for references and actually contact them! See if you can contact people who have been serviced in your neighborhood.

- Great customer service is a sign of a good professional handyman service. You should be able to speak directly with a knowledgeable individual, who will provide you with detailed scheduling and billing information. They should also provide you with information about the company's satisfaction guarantee. A follow-up is not essential, but it is a sign of an exceptional service.

- Your handyman service should provide you with a confirmed appointment and follow through.

- Use a company that has community connections, such as being a member of the Better Business Bureau, and is respected in the community.

- Even though it might take just a bit longer to find a great handyman service, you save yourself a lot of extra phone calls and hassle in the end. In the future, you can continue to rely on this trusted service for all of your home needs and hopefully whittle away at that lengthy to-do list with just a little help.

THE GREEN HOUSE EFFECT

Now that you've read this book, you know that if you change your home, you can change your life. But you can just as easily *change your home, change the world*! Making a few minor changes in your daily routine and some simple substitutes in your shopping list can make a world of difference—literally.

Using non-toxic cleaning agents and being conscientious about the amount of energy and resources that your household uses may seem insignificant, but it's not. One person can really make a difference. And, you don't have to go totally "green" to have a positive impact on the environment.

Take this example, shared by a friend. I'm sure many of you have heard about the new, highly concentrated laundry detergents. A smaller amount of product is used to do the same amount of cleaning. Well, since you need less detergent, you need less packaging. The amount of packaging (and ultimately, waste) is reduced by two-thirds! But, it doesn't stop there. Less packaging means less bulk. Less bulk means fewer truckloads. Fewer trucks means less fuel is consumed for transportation. Less fuel means fewer harmful emissions are released into the air! So by simply using concentrated laundry detergent, you actually improve the air quality of the earth for everyone!

CHANGE YOUR HOME, CHANGE THE WORLD™.

Green Thumb, Green Lungs
Not only do plants add beauty to a room, they also regulate humidity and naturally purify the air. So, add some plants—you'll be doing more than just seeing green, you'll be breathing green, too!

Bright Idea
Energy-efficient light bulbs are a must for the "green" house. Halogen bulbs may cost a bit more than regular incandescent bulbs, but they last four times as long! That definitely means savings—of energy, money, and time.

Just Concentrate
Concentrated products (such as laundry detergent) are an easy way to go green. Not only will you help save the environment, you'll save space, too!

MEET MOLL ANDERSON

I'm always curious how other people end up in certain situations, whether it's a career or a relationship. How did *they* get *there*? Sometimes their journey is not a clear-cut series of events. In fact, life often does not follow a roadmap. It's up and down, twists and turns, inside out—it's…life! I've shared some of my past with you in this book, both personal and professional. And the story of "How I Became a Lifestyle Saver" is an example of wonderful serendipity.

Believe it or not, I have Oprah to thank for getting me started as an interior designer. I was living in Nashville, I was broke, and I was ready for *something*. I had always thought about going into design, but it never quite materialized because I was too busy following the dreams other people had for me. "You should sing!", "You should model!", "You should act!" It was hard to keep up.

One day, Oprah interviewed two women authors whom I really admire, Cheryl Richardson and Debbie Ford. They said you can learn a lot about your life by looking at images that inspire you. They suggested looking through old photographs to uncover one's hidden destiny. That thought spoke to me. I immediately went to my attic and milled through boxes and boxes of old photographs. I realized that I had years of "before" and "after"

photos. I had hundreds of photos of homes that I had "done" for my friends and for myself. At that moment, I realized that my destiny was shown in those pictures. I knew I wanted to become a designer, so I got a job in a local furniture store. From there, I got one "real" project, then another, then another. And the rest is history, though it's still unfolding. I'm not done yet!

At the time it was all happening, I might not have understood the reasons behind it, but somehow it's all worked out. Considering how much of a homebody I am, it's a miracle I ventured outside my comfort zone. But if I can do it, so can you.

What are you waiting for?